Brick Math Series

TEACHING
ADDITION
USING
LEGO® BRICKS

Dr. Shirley Disseler

COMPASS

Teaching Addition Using LEGO® Bricks

Brigantine Media/Compass Publishing
211 North Avenue
St. Johnsbury, Vermont 05819
Phone: 802-751-8802
Fax: 802-751-8804
E-mail: neil@brigantinemedia.com
Website: www.compasspublishing.org
www.brickmath.com

ORDERING INFORMATION
Quantity sales
Special discounts for schools are available for quantity purchases of physical books and digital downloads. For information, contact Brigantine Media at the address shown above or visit www.brickmath.com.

Individual sales
Brigantine Media/Compass Publishing publications are available through most booksellers. They can also be ordered directly from the publisher.
Phone: 802-751-8802 | Fax: 802-751-8804
www.compasspublishing.org
www.brickmath.com
ISBN 978-1-9384066-5-2

CONTENTS

DEDICATION

In memory of my mother, who gave me passion for teaching children, and in honor of my dad, who continually inspires me to create!

INTRODUCTION

Addition concepts start to form long before children learn to add in school. When they begin to put things together into like and unlike sets, children are beginning to develop the basic idea of addition. Students need to learn more than simply the procedures for adding; they must understand the *why* and *how* behind the process as well. A firm understanding of the process of repeated addition leads to comprehension of multiplication, which is another reason to be sure that young learners build a foundation for future math with strong addition skills.

The vocabulary of addition is key for students to master. Words such as *addend*, *sum*, *result*, *solution*, and *altogether* are content words that young addition learners must know. Teachers should be careful to use the term *addition symbol* rather than *plus sign* when discussing what is happening in an addition problem. "Plussing" is not a word, and the word *plus* only represents the symbol of the math, not the action. Teachers of mathematics should use the action of the math so that students can attach words to their understanding of the process of adding numbers.

The strategies garnered from mastery of early skills such as counting on, counting back, and one more than provide a strong foundation for understanding addition (Cathcart et al., 2014). Researchers have identified four distinct types of problems children need to learn to solve: join, separate, part-part-whole, and comparisons problems. These processes match the way the brain works when solving word problems. The use of direct modeling is beneficial to young learners because it provides a visual representation that leads to the understanding behind the action of the math (Cathcart et al., 2014).

Cathcart, W. George, Yvonne M. Pothier, James H. Vance, and Nadine S. Bezuk, *Learning Mathematics in Elementary and Middle Schools: A Learner-Centered Approach*. Boston: Pearson Education, 2014.

Why use LEGO® bricks to learn about addition?

LEGO® bricks help students learn mathematical concepts through modeling. If a student can model a math problem and then be able to understand and explain the model, he or she will begin the computational process without struggling. Using LEGO® bricks to model addition helps show the action of addition so that students can visualize what is happening to numbers being joined together in a problem. Modeling with LEGO® bricks is an easy way for students to demonstrate their understanding of the vocabulary and the concept of addition.

LEGO® bricks are great tools for bringing many mathematical concepts to life: basic cardinality and counting, addition and subtraction, multiplication and division, fractions, data and measurement, and statistics and probability. Using LEGO® bricks fosters discussion, modeling, collaboration, and problem solving. These are the 21st century skills that will help students learn and be globally competitive.

The use of a common child's toy to do math provides a universal language for math. Children everywhere recognize this manipulative. It's fun to learn when you're using LEGO® bricks!

HOW TO TEACH WITH THE BRICK MATH SERIES

Using the *Teaching* and *Learning* Books:
Start by taking students through the **Part 1: Show Them How** section of each chapter. Build the models, show them to the students, and ask students questions. Where directed, have students build the same models themselves so they are manipulating the bricks as you are guiding them. A document camera is helpful to display your models to the whole class as you build them. The step-by-step directions in the *Teaching* books work through several problems in Part 1. If you are using the companion *Learning* books, which are the Student Editions, have students draw their models and answer the questions in those books as you teach using the *Teaching* book.

Once students have mastered the modeling processes from Part 1, move to the **Part 2: Show What You Know** section of the chapter. Ask students to complete each of the problems using bricks and drawing their models. The companion *Learning* books (Student Editions) have space for writing answers and baseplate paper for drawing models. Move through the room and check that students are building their models correctly, drawing them clearly, and understanding the concepts being taught.

The *Learning* books (Student Editions) include an assessment for each chapter, as well as additional problems for practice and challenge. The books also include an Assessment Chart

to track each student's performance on all the skills taught in the *Addition* book.

Note: Active learning breeds active learners! Students will be motivated and engaged in math when they are using bricks. It will not be silent in your classroom, but it will be full of chatter about the math!

Suggested Bricks:

The Brick Math Series is designed to be used with basic LEGO® bricks. If you already have LEGO® bricks in your classroom, your students should be able to use them to make the models. They may have to combine smaller bricks together when the directions call for longer bricks such as 1x10s or 2x12s. Each student also needs a baseplate on which to build brick models.

Each chapter lists the bricks suggested for the lessons in that chapter for every two students, and the book includes a total brick inventory that lists all the bricks suggested for the program for every two students.

Specially designed Brick Math brick sets for one or two students are available for purchase from Brigantine Media. Brick sets are packaged in divided boxes and include a baseplate for each student.

Classroom Management Ideas:
- Before starting, have a conversation with the students about using bricks as a learning tool rather than a toy.
- Teach students the language of bricks (baseplate, stud, 1x1, 1x2, etc.).
- Assign brick sets to specific students and always give the same students the same sets. An easy way to do this is to number each brick set and assign the sets to pairs of students by number. When students know that they will always have to work with the same brick set, they are more likely to be careful that the bricks are returned to the set.
- Do not teach using bricks—or any manipulative—every day. Students also need to have opportunities to think through the math processes without having a physical object for modeling. Sometimes it helps to have students draw models without building them with bricks

first. Remember, they won't have access to manipulatives during most tests when they have to show what they have learned.

- To keep bricks clean: Put the bricks in a hosiery bag and wash them on the top rack of the dishwasher. Let them air dry. Clean bricks before assigning sets to new students.

- To keep bricks from sliding off desks, use foam shelf liner cut into rectangular pieces, or large meat trays (you can often get these free from a local supermarket).

- Inventory the sets twice a year and replace bricks as needed. There are a variety of vendors online that sell specific bricks, both new and used. LEGO® retail stores also sell a variety of individual bricks.

WHAT DOES IT MEAN TO ADD?

SUGGESTED BRICKS

Size	Number
1x1	20
1x2	10
1x3	8
1x4	8
1x6	4
1x10	4
2x2	8
2x3	6
2x4	6
2x6	4

Note: Using a baseplate will help keep the bricks in a uniform line. One large baseplate is suggested for these activities.

Students will learn/discover:
- The definition of *addition*
- What it means to add two numbers
- How to combine sets

Why is this important?

Being able to model addition and understand what it means to add will serve as a model for combining sets in multiplication. Formulating an understanding of basic addition helps students with place value when adding larger numbers.

Vocabulary:
- Add: To join or combine sets
- Sum: The combined total of two or more sets
- Addend: Terms in an addition problem
- Plus: A symbol of math that denotes addition
- Set: An individual amount with a common characteristic; one amount

How to use the companion student book, Le*arning Addition Using LEGO® Bricks*:
- After students build their models, have them draw the models and explain their thinking in the student book. Recording the models on paper after building them with bricks helps reinforce the concepts being taught.
- Discuss the vocabulary for each lesson with students as they work through the student book.
- Use the assessment in the student book to gauge student understanding of the content.

Part 1: Show Them How

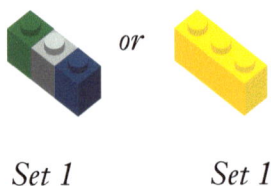

1. Build a model of the number 3 using either three 1x1 bricks or one 1x3 brick. Have students build their own models.

   Ask students what number the model represents and how they know. Students should understand that counting each stud one-to-one shows 3 studs.

   Have students draw the model and label it *Set 1*. Explain that a *set* is represented by a group of studs that model one number.

or

Set 1   *Set 1*

2. Build another model that shows the number 4. You can do this in four different ways: four 1x1 bricks, two 1x2 bricks, one 1x4 brick, or one 2x2 brick. Have students make their own models.

   Have students draw their models and label them *Set 2*.

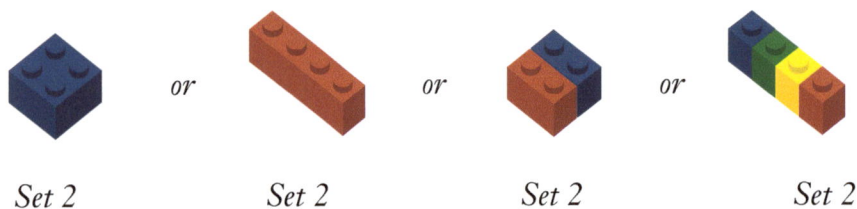

or   *or*   *or*

Set 2   *Set 2*   *Set 2*   *Set 2*

3. Ask students what would happen if one set of studs from Set 1 (representing the number 3) and one set of studs from Set 2 (representing the number 4) were combined. Students should answer that there would be 7 studs in the group. Have students build the solution model to prove the answer.

   Have students draw their solution model and label it *Set 3*.

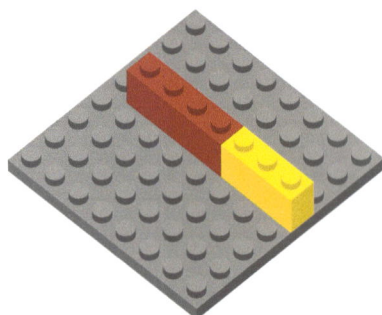

Set 3

Explain that Set 3 represents the *sum* in the problem and that Sets 1 and 2 represent the *addends*. Show students a drawing of the brick model with the brick sets separated slightly, with a box between them that has an addition symbol in it.

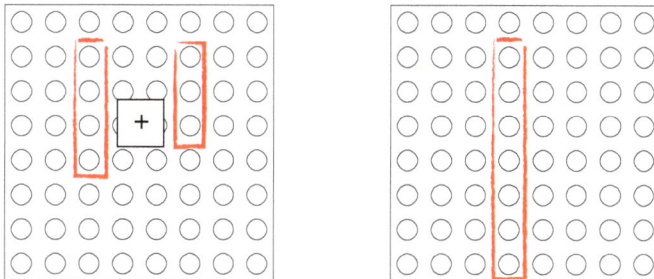

Explain to students that the box between sets 1 and 2 is where we show the action of the math, using the addition symbol (+). Tell students that although this is sometimes called a "plus sign," it's better to name it using the action of the math—addition.

Note: Be careful not to call the *addition symbol* the "plus sign," because it is not always referred to with that terminology. This can cause vocabulary issues on standardized tests.

Show students how to write a mathematical statement for their model: 3 + 4 = 7

Have students write the mathematical statement.

4. Review the terms *set*, *add*, *addend*, and *sum* using the models.

5. Have students build a model of the number 8 using studs. Remind students that they are counting studs, not bricks.

Build a model of the number 8. Show students your model and ask how their models are like yours and different from yours. Remind them that 8 can be made many ways and list some of them (3 + 5; 4 + 4; 7 + 1; 6 + 2, 3 + 5, etc.)

Have students draw their models of 8.

Possible models

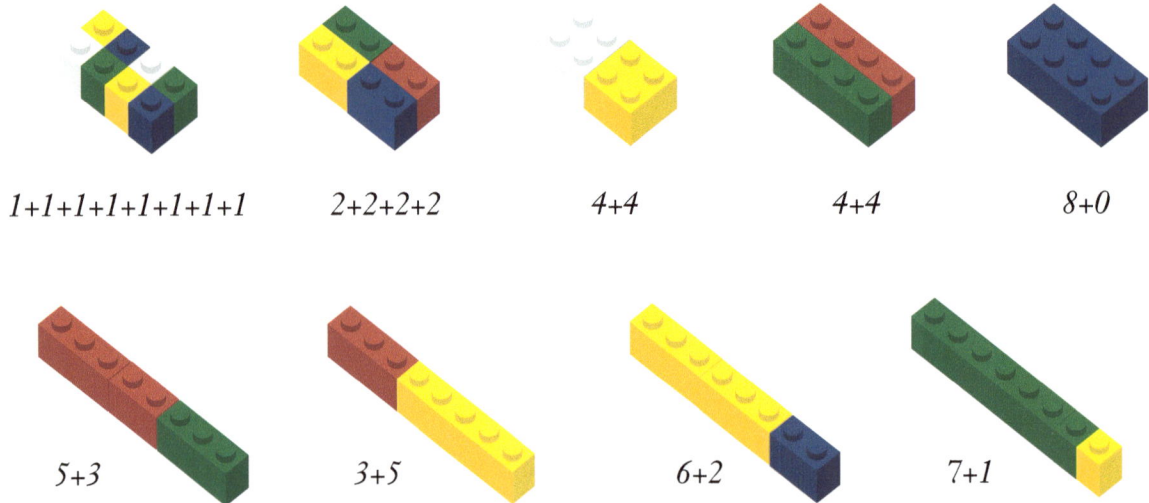

1+1+1+1+1+1+1+1	2+2+2+2	4+4	4+4	8+0

5+3	3+5	6+2	7+1

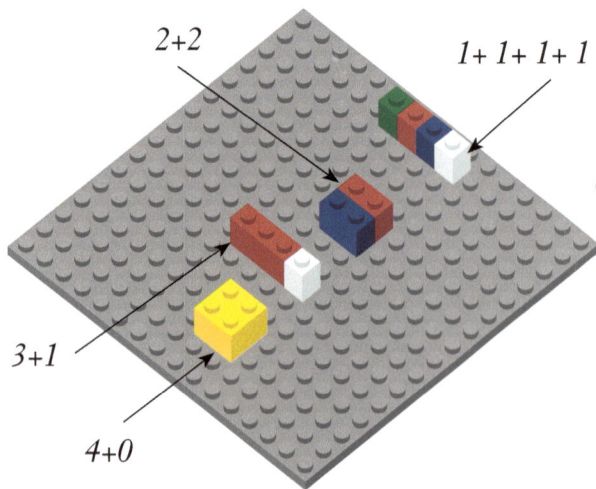

2+2

1+ 1+ 1+ 1

3+1

4+0

Possible models

6. Have students build a model of 4.

Have students draw their models of 4 on the same baseplate paper with their drawing of 8.

7. Have students draw a box between the drawings of the two sets that show 8 and 4, and then place the addition symbol in the box. Ask students what the addition symbol means. Students should understand that it shows combining the two numbers or sets into one set.

Have students combine the two numbers and make a model that shows the solution or the *sum*. The sum of 8 and 4 is 12. Have students draw their model.

Have students write a mathematical sentence for the addition problem. Students should write *8 + 4 = 12*. Have students describe or explain the action according to the steps.

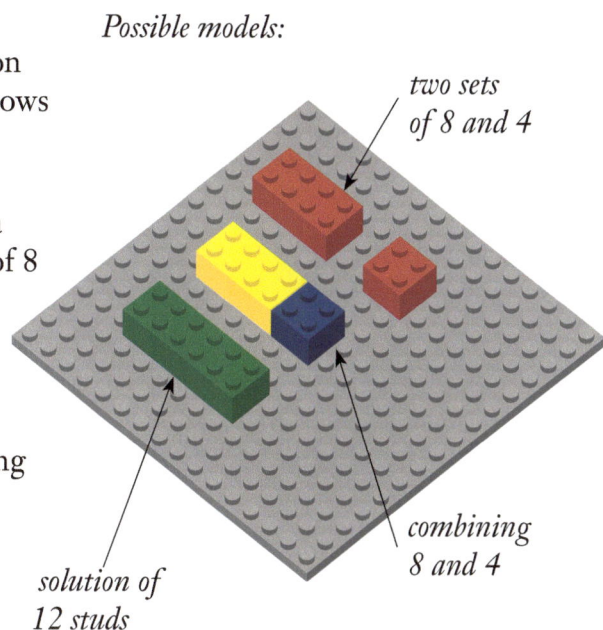

Possible models:

*two sets
of 8 and 4*

*combining
8 and 4*

*solution of
12 studs*

8. Have students model the problem *9 + 5* = _____ using the following steps:

Possible models:

- Build the number 9 with studs and build the number 5 with studs and draw the model
- Place the appropriate math symbol between the addends in the drawing
- Build a model that shows the sum of the two addends and draw the model
- Describe the model

Student should show this level of understanding: "This model shows a set of 9 and a set of 5 added together to get 14. The sum is 14. Addends are 9 and 5. Adding means to put together in one set."

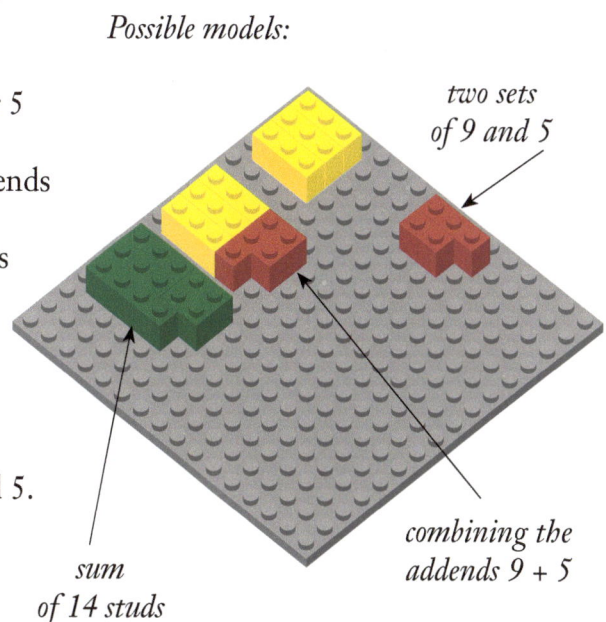

*two sets
of 9 and 5*

*combining the
addends 9 + 5*

*sum
of 14 studs*

Set 1
the number 2

Set 2
the number 6

Set 3
the sum
2 + 6 = 8

The action of
combining (addition)
2 + 6

Part 2: Show What You Know

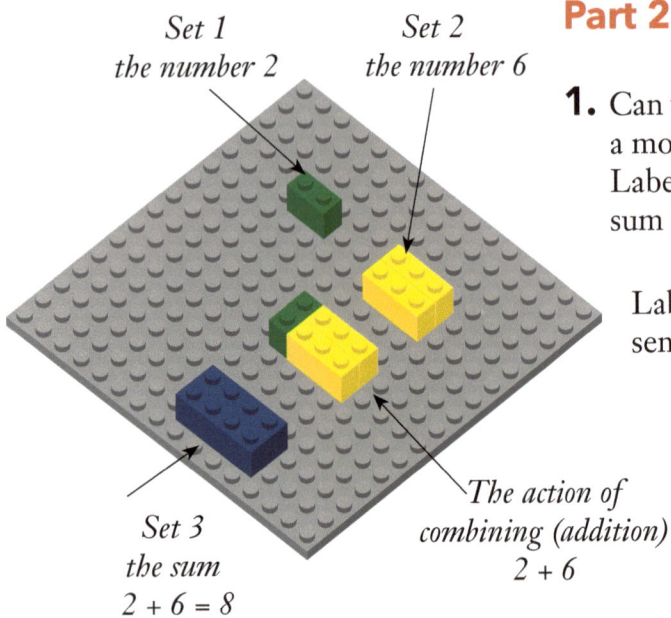

1. Can you build a model that shows the number 2 and a model that shows the number 6? Draw your model. Label the numbers *Set 1* and *Set 2*. Build *Set 3* as the sum of *Sets 1* and *2*.

Label the parts of the drawing and write a math sentence.

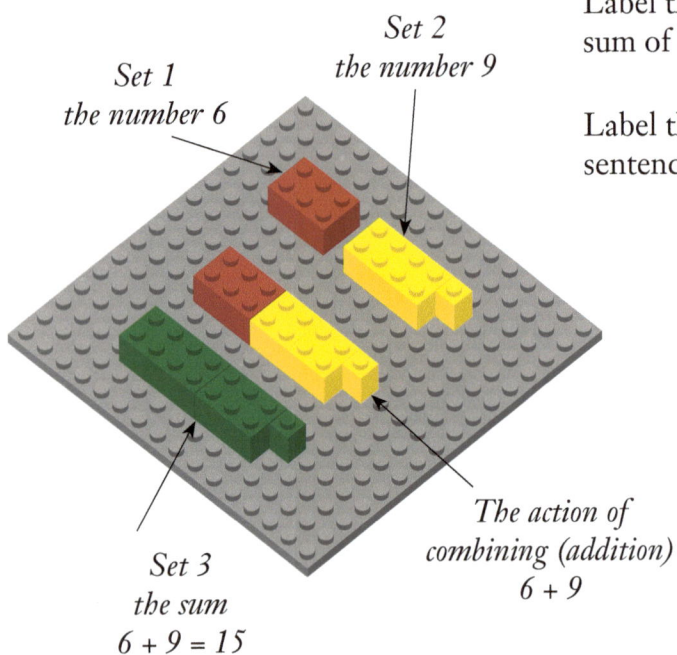

2. Can you build a model that shows the number 6 and a model that shows the number 9? Draw your model. Label the numbers *Set 1* and *Set 2*. Build *Set 3* as the sum of *Sets 1* and *2*.

Label the parts of the drawing and write a math sentence.

Set 2
the number 9

Set 1
the number 6

Set 3
the sum
6 + 9 = 15

The action of
combining (addition)
6 + 9

3. Can you build a model for this math sentence? 5 + 7 = 12

Draw and explain your model. Label all the parts of the model (addends, sum, math symbol).

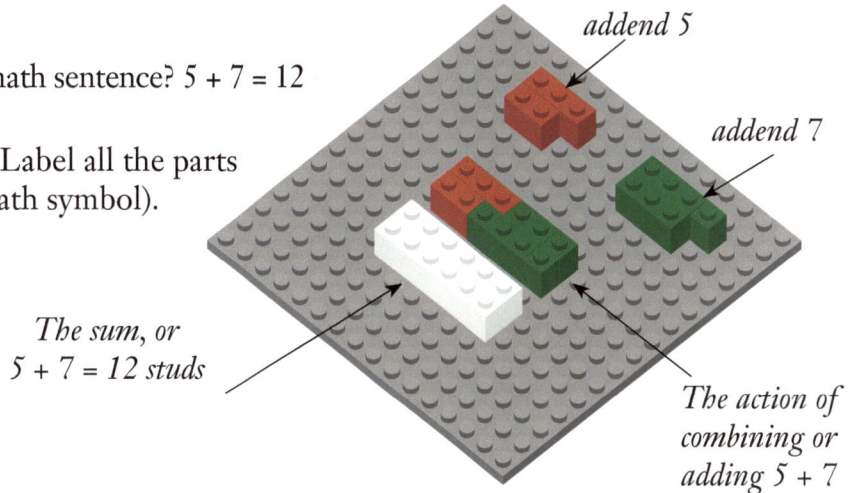

addend 5

addend 7

The sum, or 5 + 7 = 12 studs

The action of combining or adding 5 + 7

4. Can you build a model that shows 2 tens and 4 ones added to 1 ten and 2 ones? What is the sum? Show how you found the sum. Draw and explain your model. Write a math sentence for your model.

Note: The model illustrated is a ten-frame model, but more advanced students may use a place value model.

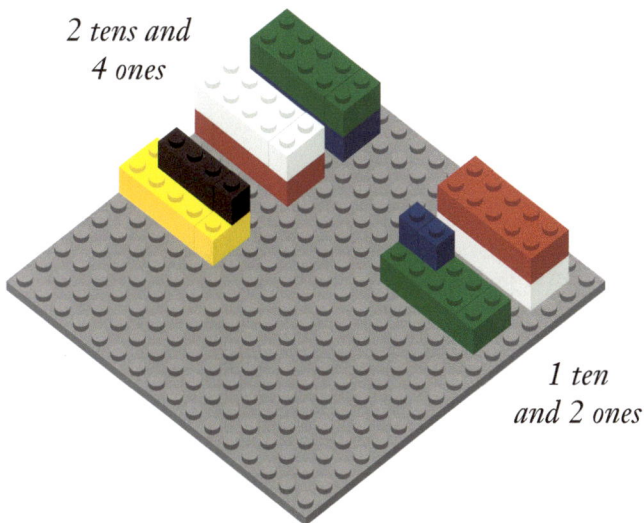

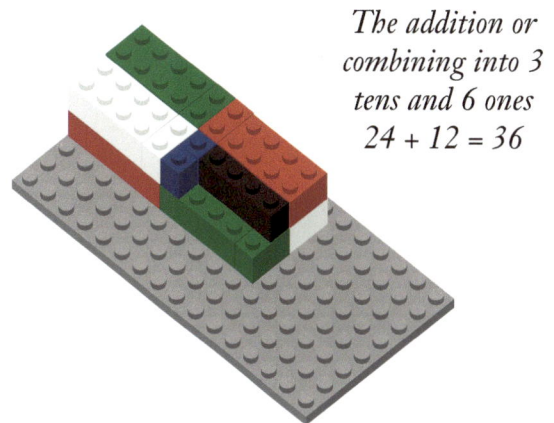

2 tens and 4 ones

1 ten and 2 ones

The addition or combining into 3 tens and 6 ones 24 + 12 = 36

Challenge:
Build a model of an addition problem. Do not include the sum in the model. Find a partner and exchange problems. Solve your partner's problem. After you have both completed the problems, discuss your solutions and make sure you can explain the model. Draw your partner's models and your solution to the model. Explain your solution in writing.

SUGGESTED BRICKS

Size	Number
1x1	10 each of 4 colors
1x2	8
1x3	6
1x4	6
1x6	4
1x8	4
1x10	4
1x12	1

Note: Using a baseplate will help keep the bricks in a uniform line. One large baseplate is suggested for these activities.

Note: There are no 5, 7 or 9-stud bricks, so students will need to use a combination of bricks to create those models.

HOW MANY WAYS?

Students will learn/discover:
- How to use multiple statements to find the same sum

Why is this important?
Being able to model sums using various addend combinations helps students develop a firm base for mental math, fact recognition, and number relationships.

Vocabulary:
- Sum
- Addend
- Equation

How to use the companion student book, *Learning Addition Using LEGO® Bricks*:
- After students build their models, have them draw the models and explain their thinking in the student book. Recording the models on paper after building them with bricks helps reinforce the concepts being taught.
- Discuss the vocabulary for each lesson with students as they work through the student book.
- Use the assessment in the student book to gauge student understanding of the content.

Part 1: Show Them How

1. Build a base model of 6 using a 1x6 brick. Have students build the same model, or display your model to the class. Explain that this model shows the sum. Ask students how many ways there are to make the number 6.

2. Begin with 1 + 5. Use two different colors of bricks for the two addends. Stack the bricks on top of the 1x6 brick to represent the 2 addends that make the sum.

Show the next two addends, 5 + 1, using different colors. Stack the bricks showing 5 + 1 on top of the model of 1 + 5. Continue building the model until all the equations that equal 6 are represented.

Have students draw the model and label all the equations represented by each row of bricks.

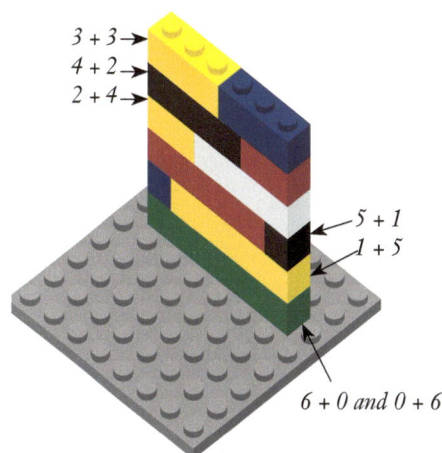

3 + 3 →
4 + 2 →
2 + 4 →

← 5 + 1
← 1 + 5

6 + 0 and 0 + 6

3. Ask students how many ways there are to make the number 8. Have students begin by placing one 1x8 brick on the baseplate to represent the number 8.

Ask students what would be the first way to make 8. Answers will vary, but try to get students in the habit of beginning with the number 1. Lead students by saying "1 plus blank equals 8," and asking students what number goes in the blank.

Have students use one 1x1 brick to represent the number 1 and find a combination of bricks in one other color that total 7 studs. Student could use a 1x3 and a 1x4 brick, or a 1x1, 1x2, and a 1x4 brick, etc. Write a math equation for this model: 1 + 7 = 8.

Have students build another layer reversing the colors. Ask students what new math equation is shown with the reversed color bricks. (7 + 1 = 8)

4. Have students continue the process until they think they have found all the ways to make 8. Ask students how they know they have all the ways to make 8. (The pattern will begin to repeat.)

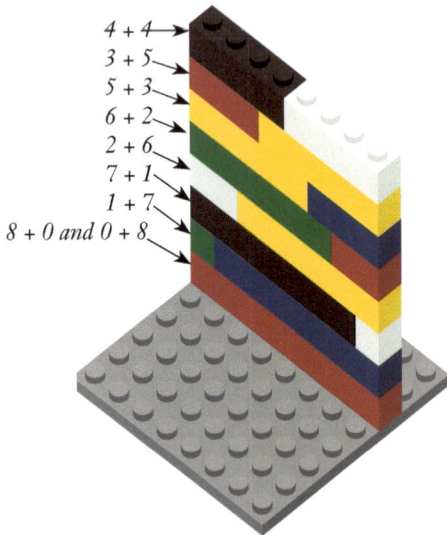

5. Have students share their models with a partner and discuss the ways to make 8. *Note:* Discuss with students that you cannot show 8 + 0 and 0 + 8 two different ways.

4 + 4
3 + 5
5 + 3
6 + 2
2 + 6
7 + 1
1 + 7
8 + 0 and 0 + 8

Part 2: Show What You Know

1. Can you build a model to show all the ways to make the sum of 4? Share your model with a partner. Draw your model and write all the math equations for your model.

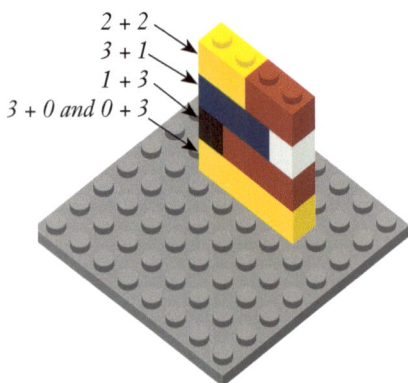

2 + 2
3 + 1
1 + 3
3 + 0 and 0 + 3

2. Can you build a model to show all the ways to make the sum of 10? Share your model with a partner. Draw your model and write all the math equations for your model.

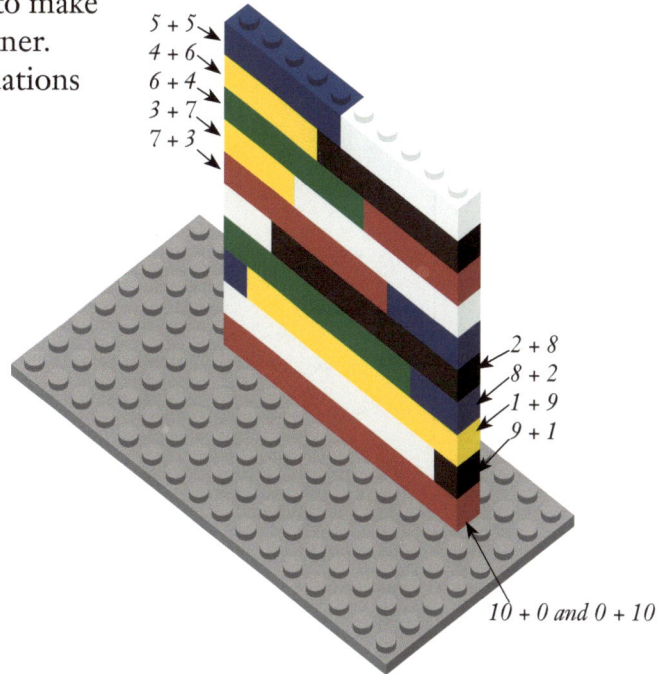

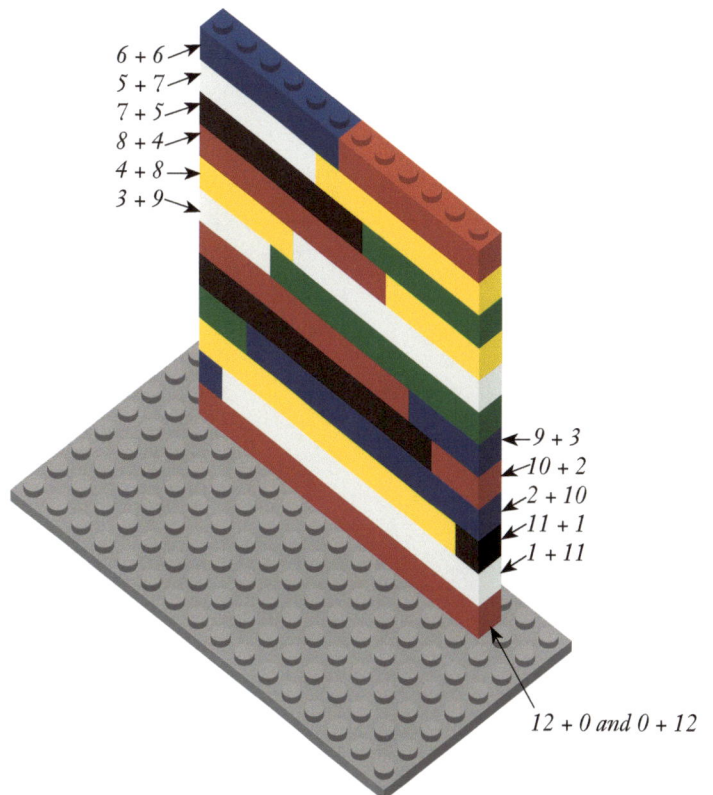

5 + 5
4 + 6
6 + 4
3 + 7
7 + 3

2 + 8
8 + 2
1 + 9
9 + 1

10 + 0 and 0 + 10

3. Can you build a model to show all the ways to make the sum of 12? Share your model with a partner. Draw your model and write all the math equations for your model.

6 + 6
5 + 7
7 + 5
8 + 4
4 + 8
3 + 9

9 + 3
10 + 2
2 + 10
11 + 1
1 + 11

12 + 0 and 0 + 12

3

SUGGESTED BRICKS

Size	Number
1x1	10 each of 4 colors
1x2	4
1x3	4
2x2	6
2x3	6
2x4	6

Note: Using a baseplate will help keep the bricks in a uniform line. One large baseplate is suggested for these activities.

TEN-FRAMES ADDITION WITHIN TWENTY

Students will learn/discover:
How to add within 20

Why is this important?
Adding numbers within 20 combines early number skills such as one-to-one correspondence with the joining of values into one set. This fosters the ability to use mental math later with regard to sets of 10.

Vocabulary:
- Ten-Frame
- Ten
- Twenty
- Addition
- Addend
- Set
- Sum

How to use the companion student book, *Learning Addition with LEGO® Bricks*:
- After students build their models, have them draw the models and explain their thinking in the student book. Recording the models on paper after building them with bricks helps reinforce the concepts being taught.
- Discuss the vocabulary for each lesson with students as they work through the student book.
- Use the assessment in the student book to gauge student understanding of the content.

Review of ten-frames from *Teaching Counting and Cardinality Using LEGO® Bricks*:

If students have not used ten-frames, teach this strategy first, and then move to the addition activities with ten-frames. *Note:* You may need to review working with ten-frames even if students learned it earlier.

1. Build two *ten-frames* on a baseplate. Show your models to the students and have them each build two ten-frames.

Note: A ten-frame has a 2x5-stud configuration, but there are no 2x5 LEGO® bricks. To build a ten-frame, use one 2x4 brick and one 1x2 brick of the same color or one 2x2 brick and one 2x3 brick of the same color.

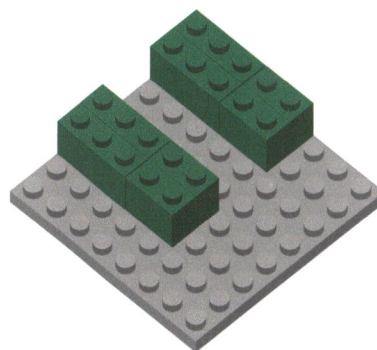

Ask students to count the number of studs in each ten-frame.

Students should count 10. Discuss with them that this model is called a *ten-frame* and is used to model numbers in sets of ten.

2. Ask students to place one 1x1 brick on top of each stud in the first ten-frame.

Students should be able to use one-to-one correspondence to count to ten. Have students draw their models.

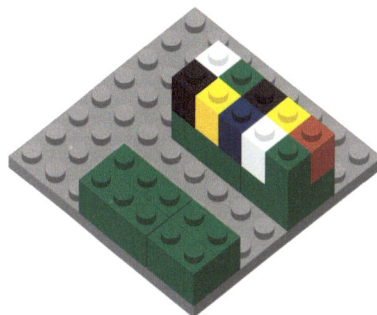

3. Ask students to place a 1x1 brick on each stud *of the top row only* of the second ten-frame. Have students write the number of studs used and draw their models.

Students should count 5 studs.

Ask students to look at both ten-frames. Have students count to determine which ten-frame models the larger number and explain why. Have students record their results in writing.

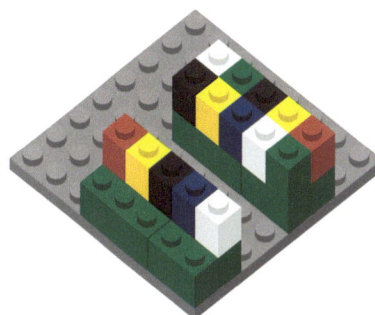

Students should say that the first ten-frame models the larger number because it shows 10 studs, while the second one shows 5 studs.

Part 1: Show Them How

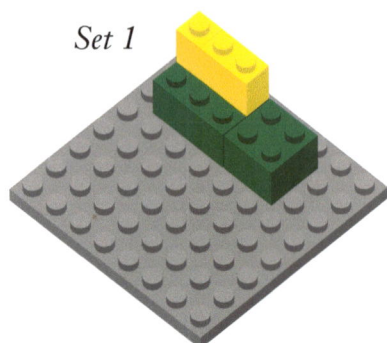

Set 1

1. Ask students to count to 3 and to show you three fingers. Tell students that they are going to begin adding numbers between 0 and 20.

Build a ten-frame. Model the number 3 on the ten-frame using three 1x1 bricks. Show students your model of the number 3 and have them build the same model. Have students count the number of studs along with you. Explain that these studs form a *set*. Call it *Set 1*, with 3 studs.

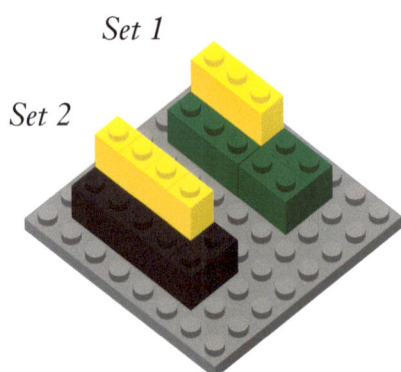

Set 1

Set 2

2. On the same baseplate, build a ten-frame with a model of the number 4 using four 1x1 bricks. Show students your model of the number 4 and have them build the same model. Have students count the number of studs along with you.

Call it *Set 2*, with 4 studs.

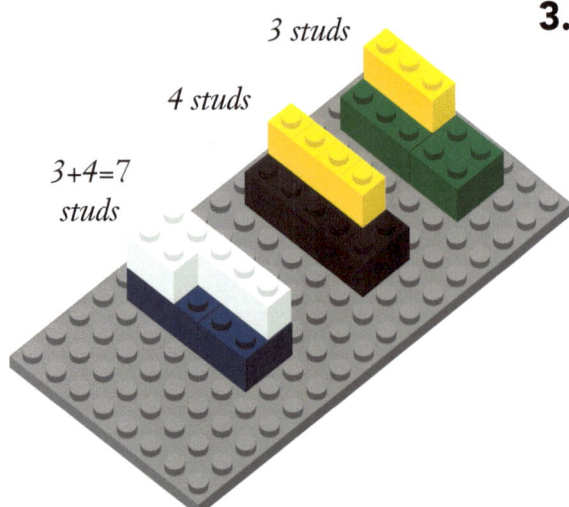

3 studs

4 studs

3+4=7 studs

3. Ask students what the model would look like if the studs of both sets are combined.

Students should answer that there would be 7 studs in the new set. Have them prove this by building a model. Show students how to write an addition sentence for the solution: $3 + 4 = 7$. Use the vocabulary: the *sum* is 7. Have students draw and label their models.

4. Have students build a model of the number 12 using ten-frames.

Have students build a model of the number 8 using another ten-frame on the same baseplate.

Have students build an addition model of 12 + 8 to prove the solution to the problem. Have students draw their models.

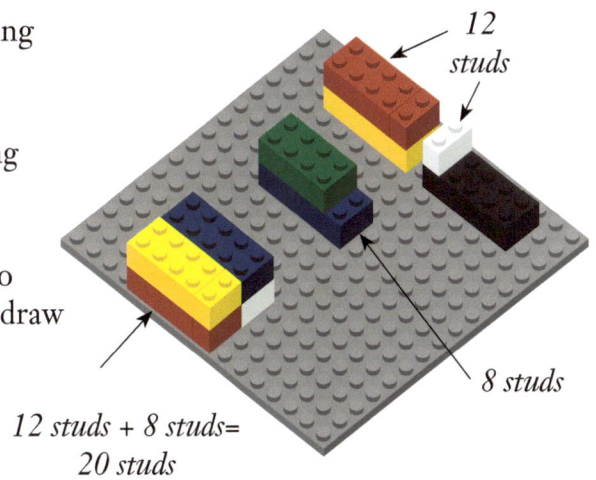

12 studs

8 studs

12 studs + 8 studs=
20 studs

Part 2: Show What You Know

1. Can you model the addition of 4 and 6 using ten-frames? Show both sets of numbers and then show how you got the solution with a third model. Draw your models and label all the parts.

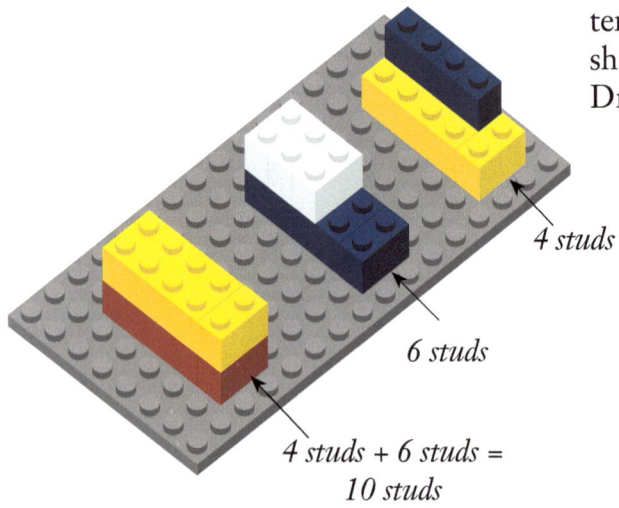

4 studs

6 studs

4 studs + 6 studs = 10 studs

2. Can you build ten-frame models of 14 + 5 and model the solution? Draw your models and label all the parts.

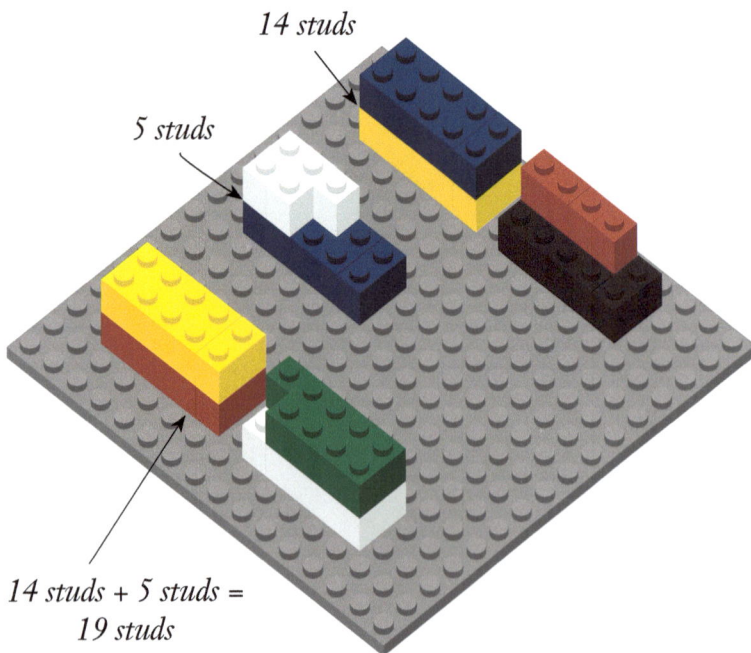

14 studs

5 studs

14 studs + 5 studs = 19 studs

3. Can you build ten-frame models of 15 + 5 and model the solution? Draw your models and label all the parts.

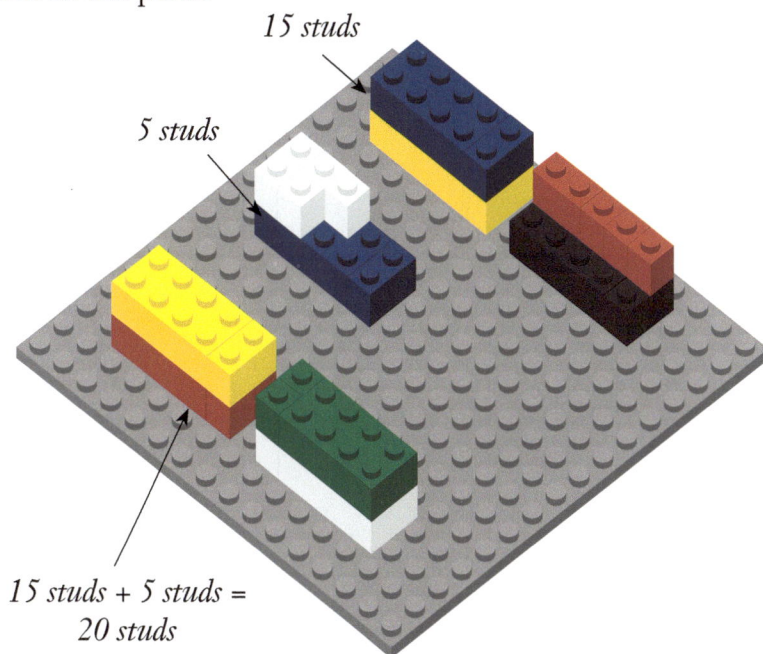

15 studs

5 studs

15 studs + 5 studs = 20 studs

4. Can you build ten-frame models of 6 + 6 and model the solution? Draw your models and label all the parts.

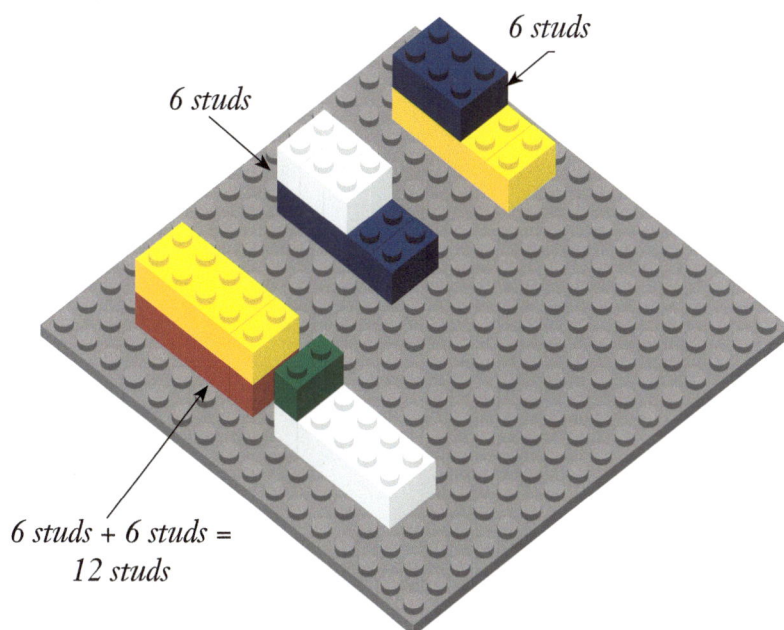

6 studs

6 studs

6 studs + 6 studs = 12 studs

4

PLACE VALUE ADDITION

Students will learn/discover:
How to model addition problems using hundreds, tens, and ones

Why is this important?
Being able to model numbers in the context of hundreds, tens, and ones helps students understand the importance of place value in computation and mental math. This skill is also important as students begin to add larger numbers in the base ten system.

Vocabulary:
- Place value
- Hundreds
- Tens
- Ones
- Addition
- Decomposing

How to use the companion student book, *Learning Addition Using LEGO® Bricks*:
- After students build their models, have them draw the models and explain their thinking in the student book. Recording the models on paper after building them with bricks helps reinforce the concepts being taught.
- Discuss the vocabulary for each lesson with students as they work through the student book.
- Use the assessment in the student book to gauge student understanding of the content.

Part 1: Show Them How

1. Show students the bricks that represent each place value, beginning with the ones place, then the tens place, and then the hundreds place.

Explain to students:
- the 1x1 brick represents the ones place because one stud represents one digit (0 to 9)
- the 1x2 brick represents tens because it shows one digit in the tens place and one zero
- the 1x3 brick represents hundreds because it shows one digit in the hundreds place and two zeros
  Have students build this model. Have students draw the model and label each brick as the ones, tens, and hundreds place.

2. Have students build the number 25 using the place value model as a guide. Have students share their model with a partner and describe the model. Have students draw and explain their models in writing.

Note: Students may choose to stack bricks to model place value, as shown in the second illustration. As long as they are correctly modeling the place value concept, this is acceptable.

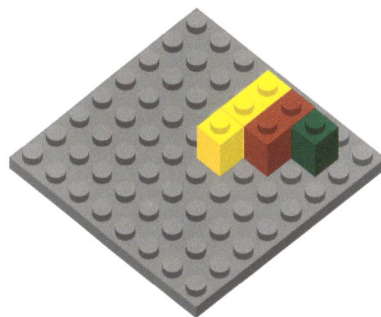

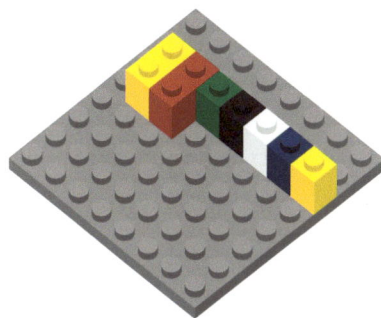

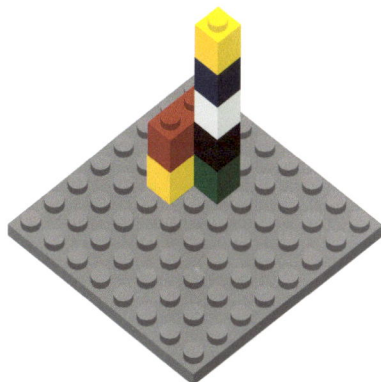

Possible models

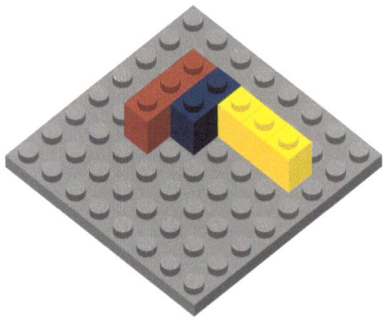

3. Have students model the number 123 and discuss their models with a partner. Have each student draw his/her model and write the expanded form that the bricks represent.

Students should understand that the 1x3 brick represents 100, the two 1x2 bricks represent 10 + 10 = 20, and the three 1x1 bricks represent 1 + 1 + 1 = 3.

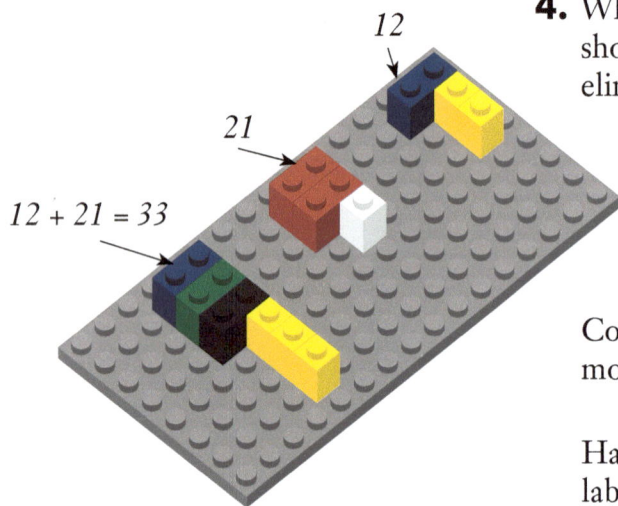

4. When all students understand how to model place value, show them how place value is used in addition by modeling 12 + 21.

Build a place value model for 12 using tens and ones, and build a place value model for 21 using tens and ones.

Combine all the bricks in the two models into a third model that shows the addition.

Have students build the same models, then draw and label them.

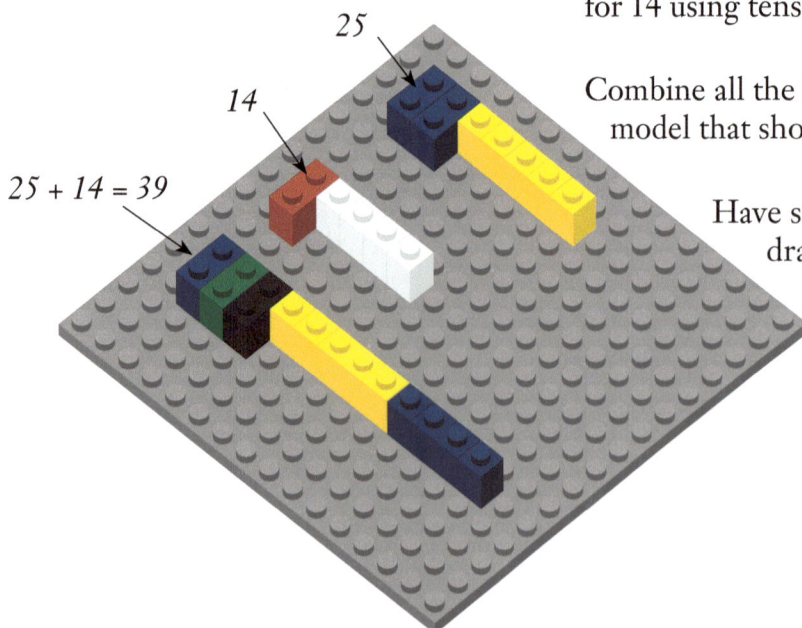

5. Use place value modeling to show 25 + 14. Build the model for 25 using tens and ones, and build the model for 14 using tens and ones.

Combine all the bricks in the two models into a third model that shows the addition.

Have students build the same models, then draw and label them. Have students write the expanded form.

Part 2: Show What You Know

1. Can you build the number 212 using place value modeling? Draw your model and explain your thinking.

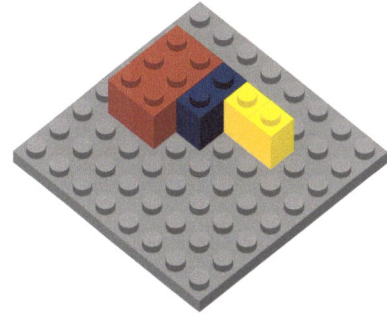

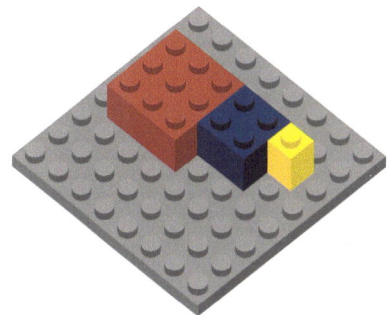

Two 1x3 bricks show 200
One 1x2 brick shows 10
Two 1x1 bricks show 2
200 + 10 + 2 = 212

2. Can you build the number 321 using place value modeling? Draw your model and explain your thinking.

Three 1x3 bricks show 300
Two 1x2 bricks show 20
One 1x1 brick shows 1
300 + 20 + 1 = 321

3. Can you build a model that shows the addition of 212 and 321? Draw your model and explain your thinking.

Write an addition sentence for your model.

300 + 200 + 10 + 10 + 10 + 1 + 1 + 1
500 + 30 + 3
533
212 + 321 = 533

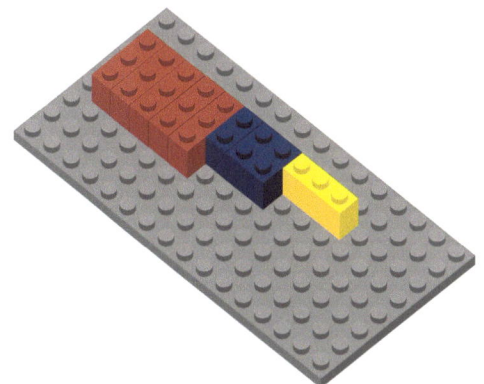

13

12

13 + 12 = 25

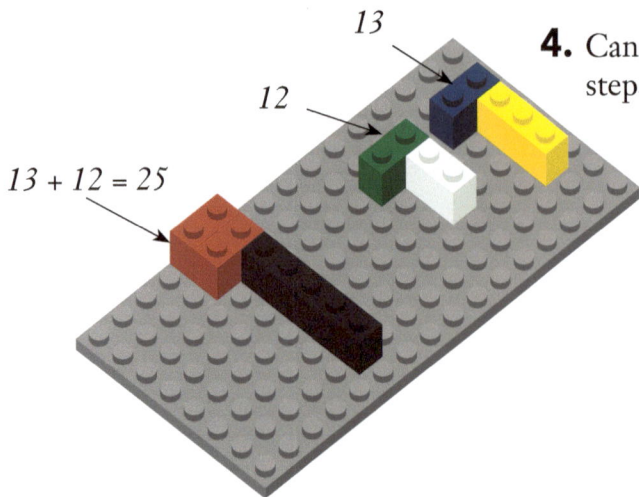

4. Can you build a model that shows 13 + 12? Show all the steps. Draw and explain your model.

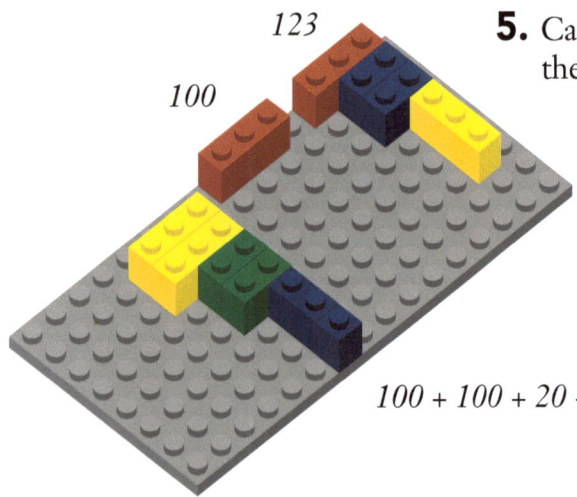

123

100

100 + 100 + 20 + 3 = 223

5. Can you build a model that shows 123 + 100? Show all the steps. Draw and explain your model.

6. Partner Problem:

Choose a partner. Each person builds a model of a number using place value modeling. Compare your number models. Add the two numbers together. Build a model that shows the addition of both numbers. Draw your model and show your solution.

Solutions will vary.

DECOMPOSING NUMBERS

Students will learn/discover:
- How to add numbers up to the sum of 20 using decomposing within 20

Why is this important?

Adding numbers up to the sum of 20 using the method of decomposing numbers in place value is key with larger numbers, up to the millions, in upper elementary grades. Linking place value to addition and decomposing numbers is important in understanding the way addition is related to other operations.

Vocabulary:
- Add
- Sum
- Addend
- Decompose
- Compose
- Expanded form

How to use the companion student book, *Learning Addition Using LEGO® Bricks*:
- After students build their models, have them draw the models and explain their thinking in the student book. Recording the models on paper after building them with bricks helps reinforce the concepts being taught.
- Discuss the vocabulary for each lesson with students as they work through the student book.
- Use the assessment in the student book to gauge student understanding of the content.

Tens place

Ones place

Part 1: Show Them How

1. Build the model shown using two 1x10 bricks or the equivalent in smaller bricks, and show it to the students.

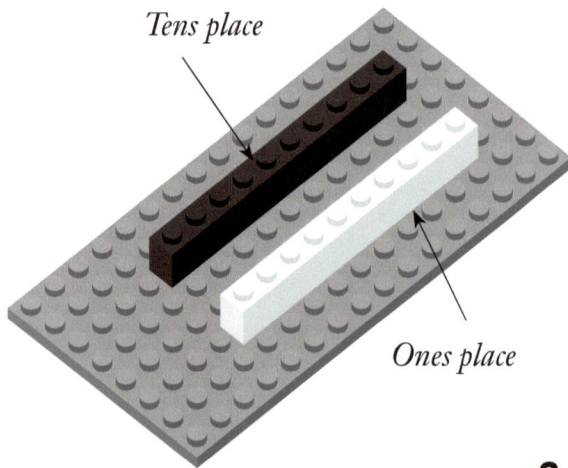

Explain that the strip on the right represents the ones place and the strip on the left represents the tens place. *Note:* This is not the same type of modeling as in Chapter 4 (Place Value Addition).

Have students build this model and draw the outlines of each brick strip on baseplate paper.

2. Describe this contextual situation to students: John has 4 cookies and Samantha has 9 cookies. How many cookies do John and Samantha have altogether?

Ask students to write the math sentence for this problem.

Students should write *4 + 9 =* ☐. Use the vocabulary and explain that 4 and 9 are *addends*.

3. Ask students to use the ones strip and build a model with bricks that show the number of John's cookies.

Students should place four 1x1 bricks (or two 1x2 bricks to represent 4 if they have mastered one-to-one correspondence) on the ones place strip to show John's 4 cookies. Have students draw their model of John's cookies.

Ask students to find bricks to model Samantha's 9 cookies in the problem and place them to the side on the baseplate, not on the strips. Students can choose nine 1x1 bricks or a combination of bricks equivalent to nine studs.

Note: It is helpful if students choose different color bricks to represent John's and Samantha's cookies.

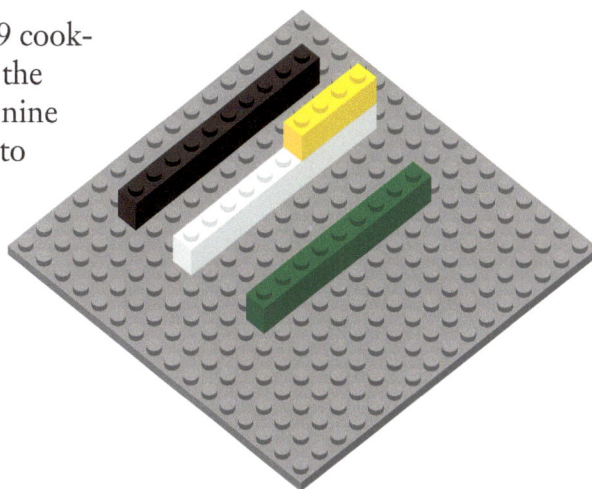

4. Ask students to add Samantha's cookies to John's cookies in the model by counting them forward or adding on. When the strip is full, explain that they now have ten and the number has to be "decomposed" to make 1 ten on the tens strip.

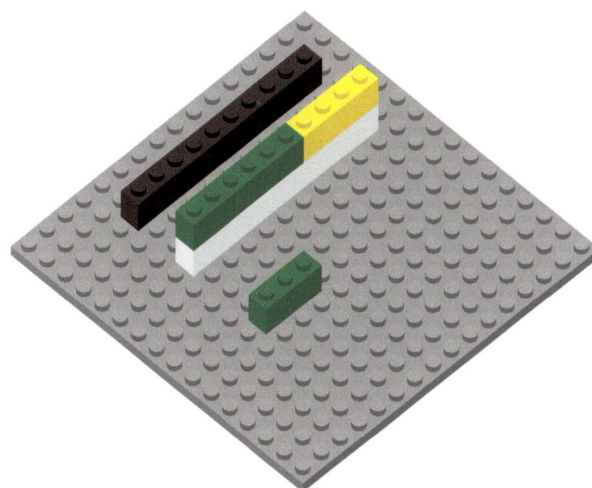

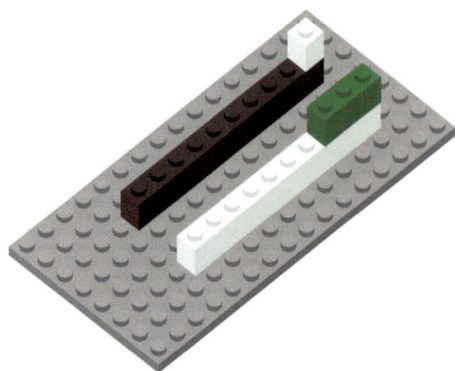

5. Remove the ten studs on the ones strip and decompose it into one set of ten displayed by one 1x1 brick on the tens place strip. Move the 3 bricks left over from Samantha's 9 cookies to the ones strip. Explain to the students that the model now shows 1 ten and 3 ones.

Have students draw the final solution model and explain their thinking. Be sure they record the total number of cookies John and Samantha have altogether. Students should write the math sentence 4 + 9 = 13.

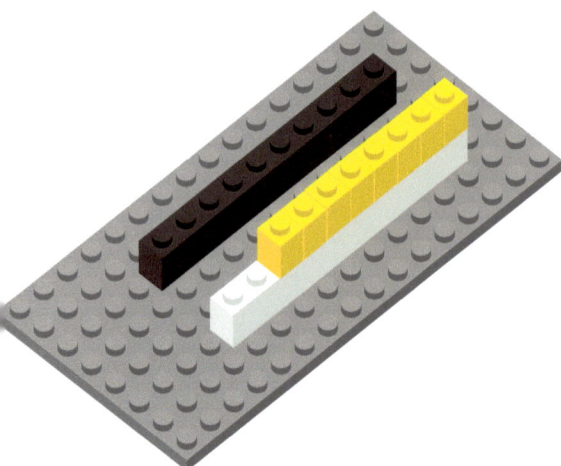

6. Have students build another two-strip model with 1x10 bricks or the equivalent and draw their models. Describe the following contextual situation: There were 8 people in line at the store. Nine more people got in line behind them. How many people were in line at the store in all?

Ask students how many studs need to be placed on the ones place strip to represent the first group in line. Students should answer "eight studs." Ask students to add bricks to the strip to show the number in line in the first part of the problem. Have students draw this part of the model.

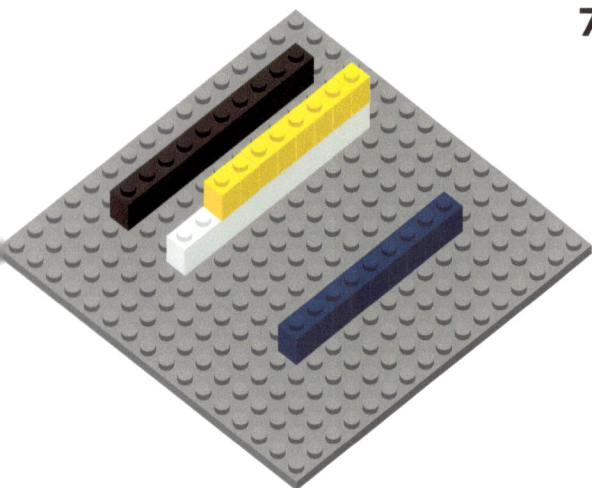

7. Ask students how many more studs are needed to represent the people who joined the line. Students should answer "nine studs." Have students select nine studs, but not put them on the strips yet.

8. Ask students to add studs to the model until the ones strip is full. When the strip is full, ask students what they need to do to continue modeling the problem.

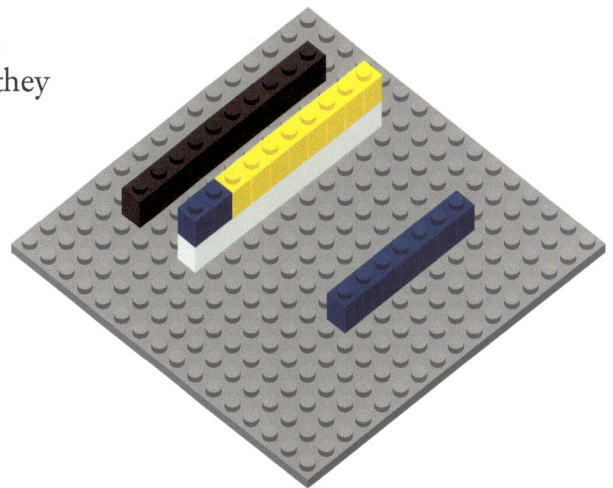

Students should understand that they should decompose the ones place and move the 1 ten to the tens strip, showing it with a new stud (a different color helps here).

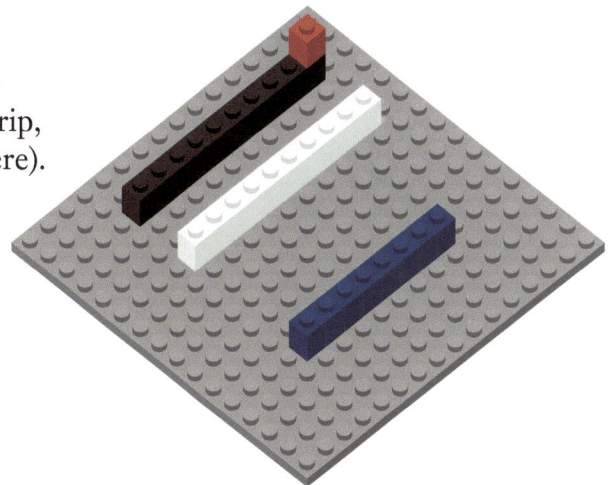

9. Ask students to show the final solution by building the ones strip. Have students draw the model, write an equation for the problem (8 + 9 = 17) and explain their thinking.

Note: You can use this opportunity to discuss expanded form if students are ready for the concept. If so, show students that the sum can be written as 1 ten + 7 ones or 10 + 7 = 17.

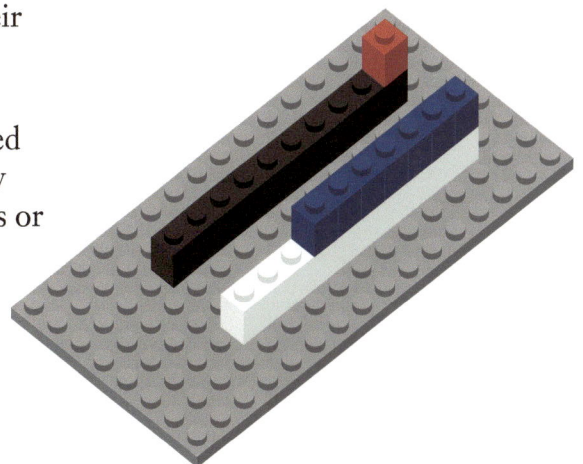

10. Have students build another two-strip model. Describe this contextual situation: Savannah had 6 pencils. Christen gave her 7 more. How many pencils did Savannah have altogether?

Ask students:
- What are the two addends in this problem? *Answer:* 6 and 7
- What math symbol should we use to write this problem? *Answer:* the addition symbol (+)
- What is the answer to this problem called? *Answer:* the sum

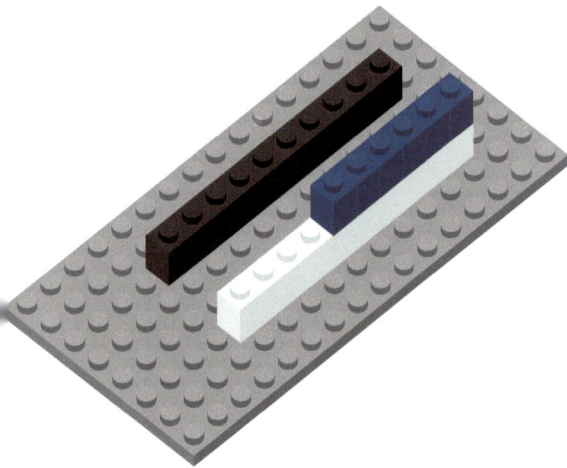

11. Ask students where the first addend studs should be placed. Students should answer that they go on the ones strip on the right. Have students build the first addend on the strip model and ask how many studs show the first addend. Students should answer "six studs."

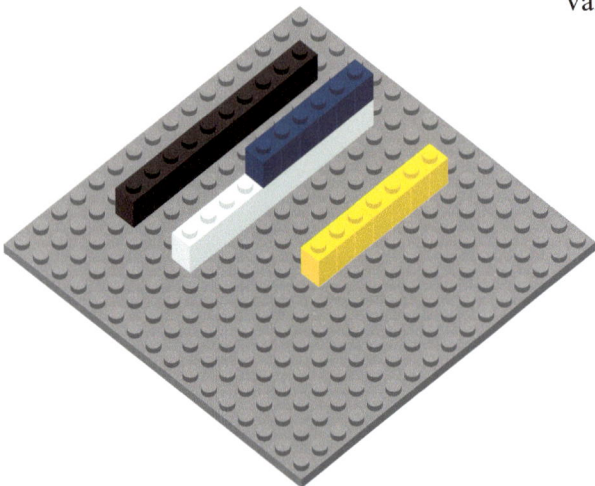

12. Ask students to select the studs that represent the second addend and put them on the baseplate, not the place value strip yet. Students should select seven studs.

Ask students to add the studs that show the extra pencils to the ones strip.

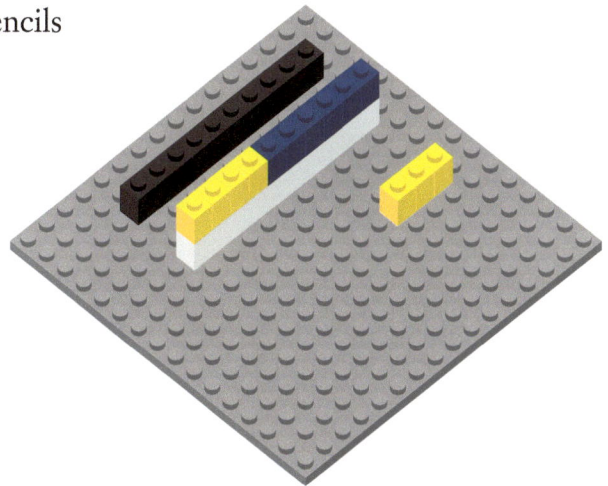

13. When they fill up the ones strip, ask students to decompose the 10 ones into 1 ten and place one new stud on the tens strip, and then bring over the rest of the studs to the ones strip.

Ask students to write an equation to show the solution.
Answer: 6 + 7 = 13

Ask students to write expanded form of the sum.
Answer: 1 tens + 3 ones = 13

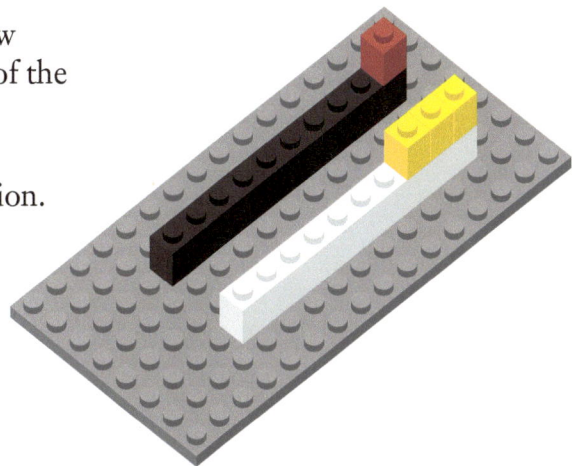

Possible solution:

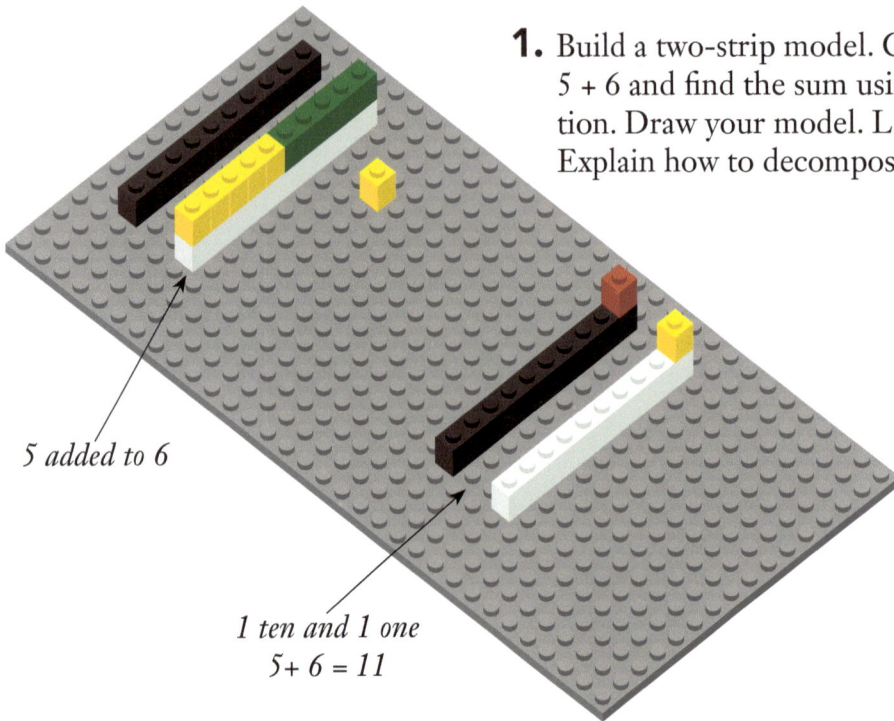

5 added to 6

1 ten and 1 one
5 + 6 = 11

Part 2: Show What You Know

1. Build a two-strip model. Can you show the problem 5 + 6 and find the sum using bricks? Write the equation. Draw your model. Label the addends and the sum. Explain how to decompose and create tens.

2. Steven has 4 pennies and 7 dimes. How many coins does Steven have in all? Build a model to show the total number of coins. Write the equation for your problem. Draw your model and explain your thinking. Write the expanded form of this problem.

10 + 1 = 11 (expanded form)
4 + 7 = 11 (equation)

Possible solution:

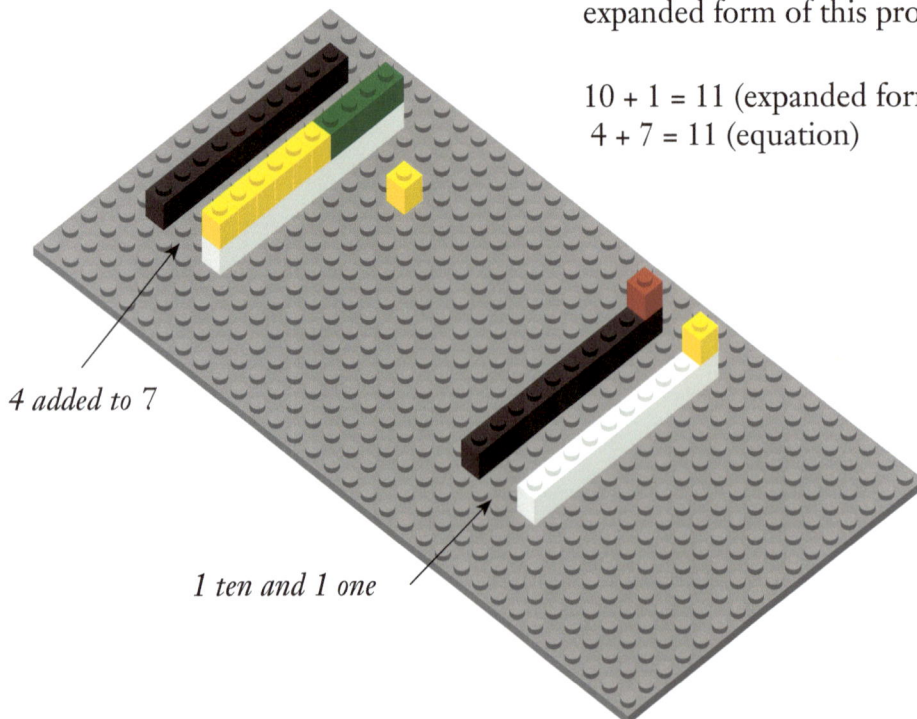

4 added to 7

1 ten and 1 one

3. There were 12 cars in the parking lot at 6:00 pm. Five more cars arrived at 6:30 pm. How many cars were in the lot in all?

Build a strip model to show the addends.

Model the addition.

Write an equation for your model. Write the expanded form for the sum. Explain your thinking.

Note: This model could be built without decomposing, since 12 can be modeled as one ten and 2 ones at the start. Students might try placing 12 single studs first, then decomposing into 1 ten and 2 ones. The purpose of this problem is to see if students can discern when they must decompose and when they do not need that strategy.

Possible solution:

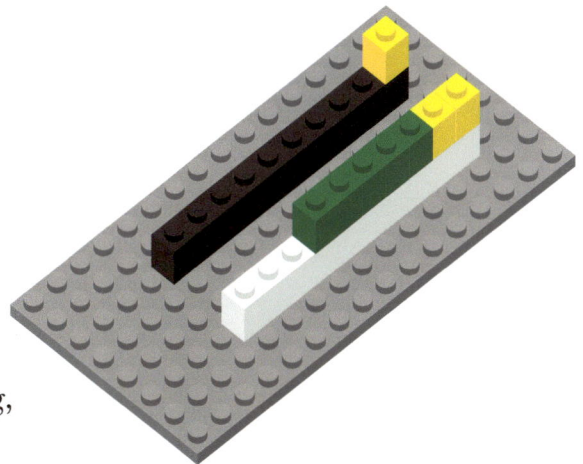

$12 + 5 = 17$ *(equation)*
$10 + 7 = 17$ *(expanded form)*

6

SUGGESTED BRICKS

Size	Number
1x1	10 each of 4 colors
1x2	6
1x3	6
1x4	5
2x2	5
2x3	5
2x4	5
1x10	3

Note: Using a baseplate will help keep the bricks in a uniform line. One large baseplate is suggested for these activities.

Note: The bricks used in these exercises may vary depending on students' ability to count. For example, if a student can see that a 1x3 brick is the same as three 1x1 bricks, they may use either configuration to show the number 3.

RESULT UNKNOWN PROBLEMS

Students will learn/discover:
- How to use a model to find the missing sum in a problem

Why is this important?
Being able to model numbers helps students formulate an understanding for number recognition. Ten-frames provide a base for seeing more than and less than ten, which helps build conceptual understanding about addition and subtraction.

Vocabulary:
- Ten-Frame
- Result
- Sum
- Addend

How to use the companion student book, *Learning Addition Using LEGO® Bricks*:
- After students build their models, have them draw the models and explain their thinking in the student book. Recording the models on paper after building them with bricks helps reinforce the concepts being taught.
- Discuss the vocabulary for each lesson with students as they work through the student book.
- Use the assessment in the student book to gauge student understanding of the content.

Part 1: Show Them How

1. Show students this addition problem: 2 + 6 = ☐

If vocabulary has not been discussed previously, be sure to discuss the terms *addend* and *sum* with students.

Ask students how to go about finding the missing number (*sum*) that belongs in the box.

Show students how to model the problem. Build three 1x10 strips or ten-frames that represent the three numbers in the problem (the two addends and the sum). *Note:* A ten-frame model is shown for this problem.

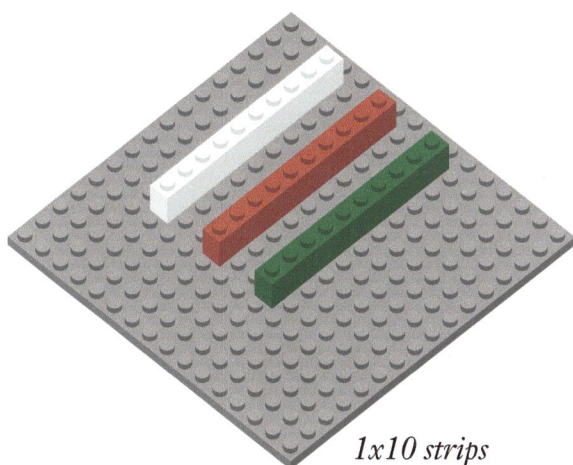

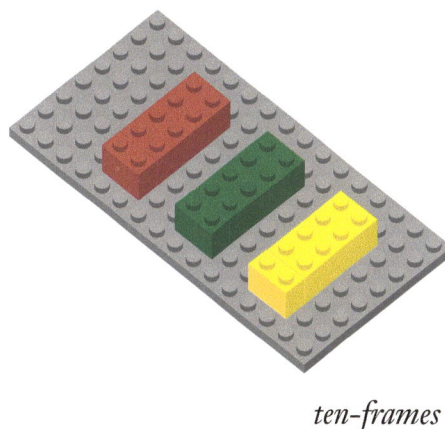

1x10 strips

ten-frames

Place 2 studs on the left ten-frame to represent the *addend* in the starting place.

Place 6 studs on the center ten-frame to represent the addend in the *change location*.

Don't place any studs on the right ten-frame to represent the missing *sum*. Using a different color to show each number may be helpful but is not a requirement.

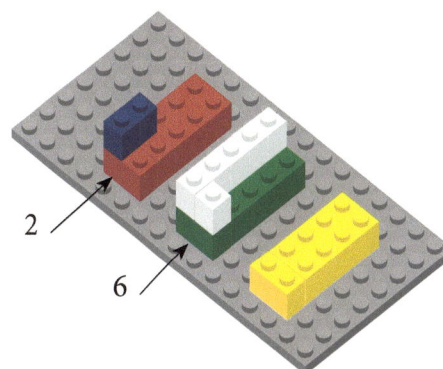

8

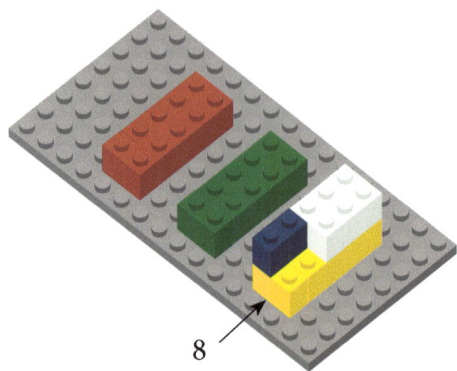

Move the bricks from the two ten-frames that represent the addends and place them on the ten-frame that represents the sum.

Show students how to use counting on to find the sum by moving the studs to the ten-frame representing the sum as you count.

Move the studs from the ten-frame that represents the first addend to the ten-frame that represents the sum and count "1, 2."

Move the studs from the center ten-frame representing the change addend to the ten-frame representing the sum and count "3, 4, 5, 6, 7, 8." Make it clear that the last stud counted represents the sum of 8.

Have students draw the model of the addends and the sum and label each part of the problem.

Have students write the math sentence: 2 + 6 = 8

2. Show students this addition problem: 3 + 6 = ☐

Ask students how to find the missing number (*sum*) that belongs in the box.

Show students how to model the problem. Build three 1x10 strips or ten-frames to represent the three numbers in the problem (the two addends and the sum). *Note*: A ten-frame model is shown for this problem.

3

6

Place 3 studs on the left ten-frame to represent the addend in the starting place.

Place 6 studs on the center ten-frame to represent the addend in the change location.

Don't place any studs on the right ten-frame to represent the missing sum. Using a different color for each number may be helpful but is not a requirement.

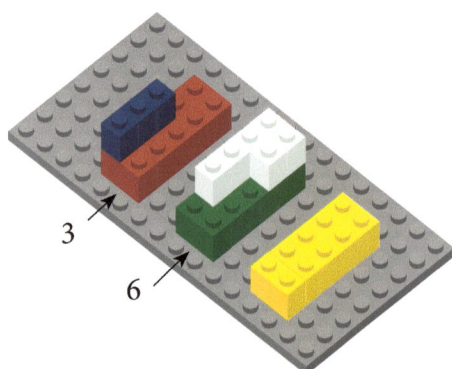

Show students how to use counting on to find the sum by moving the studs to the ten-frame representing the sum as you count.

Move the studs from the ten-frame that represents the first addend to the ten-frame that represents the sum and count "1, 2, 3."

Move the studs from the center ten-frame representing the change addend to the ten-frame representing the sum and count "4, 5, 6, 7, 8, 9." Make it clear that the last stud counted represents the sum of 9.

Have students draw the model of each part of the math sentence, label each of the parts, and write the math sentence: 3 + 6 = 9

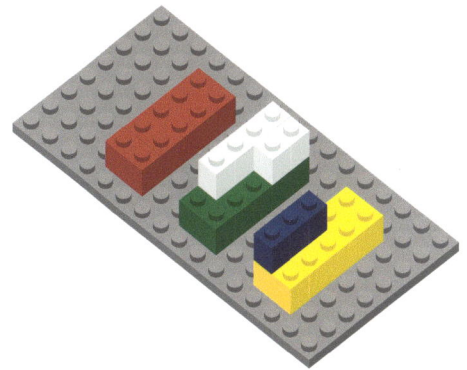

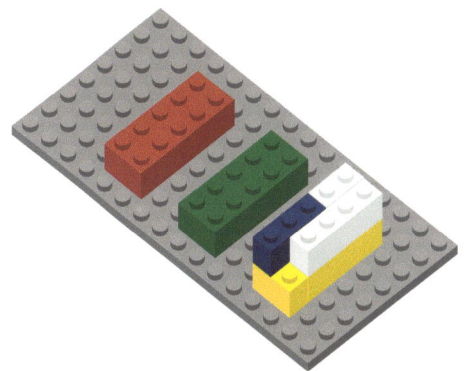

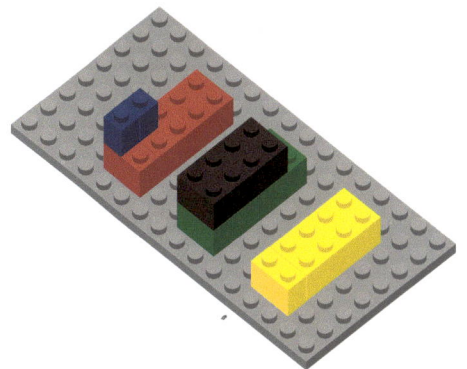

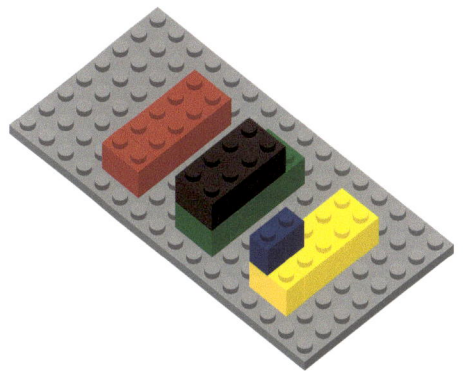

3. Show students the following problem: 2 + 8 = ☐

Have students build either a ten-frame model or a 1x10 strip model. *Note:* a ten-frame model is shown for this problem.

Place 2 studs on the model in the location of the start addend.

Place 8 studs on the model in the location of the change addend.

Leave the brick in the sum location empty to show the missing sum.

Have students model the addends and draw the model.

Ask students how to determine the sum of this math sentence. Move the studs representing the first addend to the ten-frame representing the sum and count "1, 2."

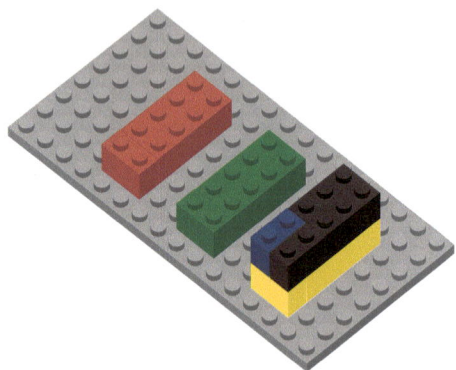

Move the 8 studs from the center ten-frame representing the change addend to the ten-frame representing the sum and count on: "3, 4, 5, 6, 7, 8, 9, 10."

Make it clear that the last stud counted is the sum of 10.

Have students draw the model of each part of the math sentence, label each of the parts, and write the math sentence.

Part 2: Show What You Know

Suggested solution:

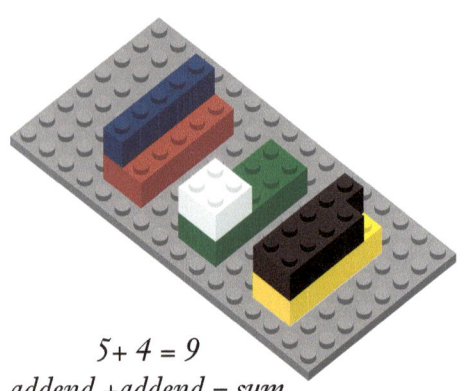

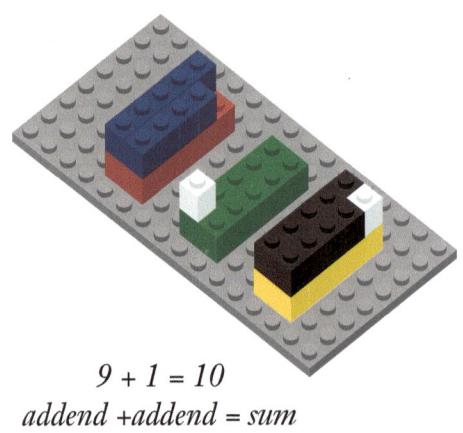

$$5 + 4 = 9$$
addend +addend = sum

1. Can you build a model that shows this math sentence?

$5 + 4 = \boxed{}$

Use either a 1x10 strip model or a ten-frame model. Draw your model and show each part of the whole.

What is the sum? Explain how you proved it with your model.

Label each part of the math sentence using the terms *addend* and *sum*.

Suggested solution:

$$9 + 1 = 10$$
addend +addend = sum

2. Can you build a model that shows this math sentence?

$9 + 1 = \boxed{}$

Use either a 1x10 strip model or a ten-frame model. Draw your model and show each part of the whole.

What is the sum? Explain how you proved it with your model.

Label each part of the math sentence using the terms *addend* and *sum*.

3. Can you build a model that shows this math sentence?

$3 + 5 = \boxed{}$

Use either a 1x10 strip model or a ten-frame model. Draw your model and show each part of the whole.

What is the sum? Explain how you proved it with your model.

Label each part of the math sentence using the terms *addend* and *sum*.

Suggested solution:

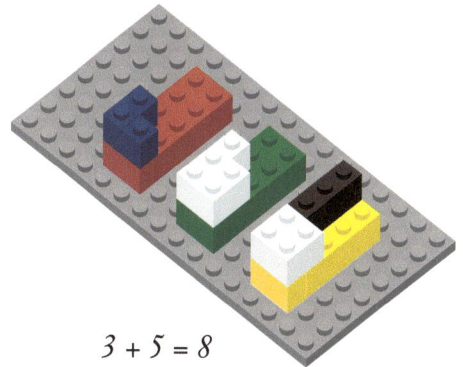

$3 + 5 = 8$
addend +addend = sum

4. Challenge: Build a model to show $5 + 6 = \boxed{}$

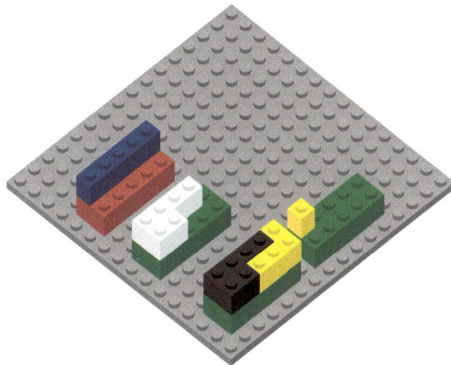

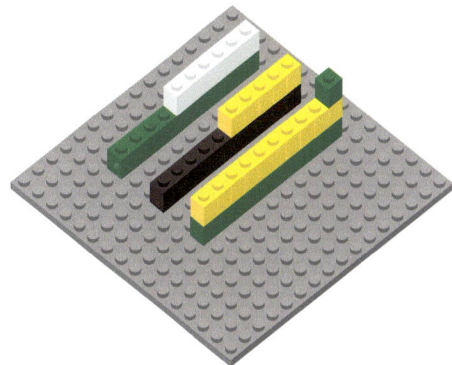

7

SUGGESTED BRICKS

Size	Number
1x1	10 each of 4 colors
1x2	6
1x3	6
1x4	5
2x2	5
2x3	5
2x4	5
1x10	3

Note: Using a baseplate will help keep the bricks in a uniform line. One large baseplate is suggested for these activities.

Note: The bricks used may vary depending on students' ability to count. For example, if a student can see that a 1x3 brick is the same as three 1x1 bricks, they may use either configuration to show the number 3.

CHANGE UNKNOWN PROBLEMS

Students will learn/discover:
- How to model problems with a missing addend in the change location, which is the second addend or value in the problem.

Why is this important?
Modeling problems with missing addends in different locations helps students understand the part-part-whole relationships between numbers. In the *change unknown* problem, students find the missing addend through a variety of strategies.

Vocabulary:
- Add
- Change unknown
- Addend
- Sum

How to use the companion student book, *Learning Addition Using LEGO® Bricks*:
- After students build their models, have them draw the models and explain their thinking in the student book. Recording the models on paper after building them with bricks helps reinforce the concepts being taught.
- Discuss the vocabulary for each lesson with students as they work through the student book.
- Use the assessment in the student book to gauge student understanding of the content.

Part 1: Show Them How

1. Show students this addition problem: 4 + ☐ = 7

If vocabulary has not been discussed previously, be sure to use and define the terms *addend*, *change unknown*, and *sum*.

Ask students how to go about finding the missing number (*addend*) that belongs in the box.

Show students how to model the problem. Build three 1x10 strips or ten-frames that represent the three numbers in the problem (the two addends and the sum). *Note:* ten-frame models are shown for this problem.

1x10 strips

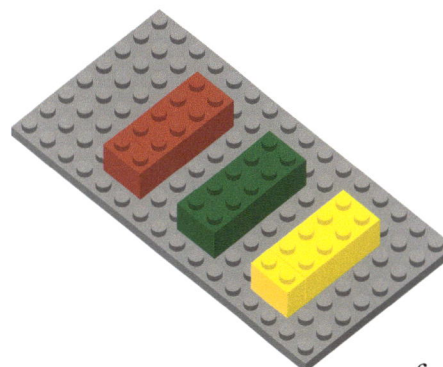

ten-frames

Place 4 studs on the left ten-frame to represent the *addend* in the starting place.

Do not place any studs on the center ten-frame to represent the missing addend in the *change location*.

Place 7 studs on the right ten-frame to represent the *sum*.

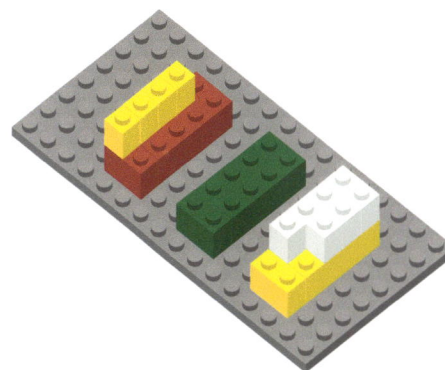

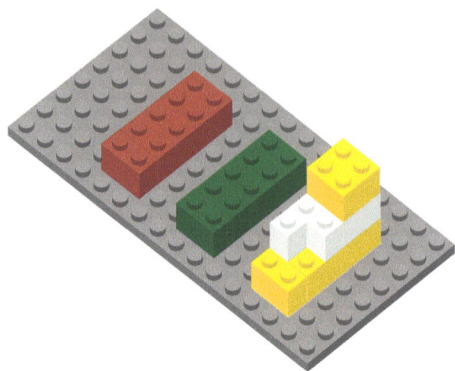

Ask students how to determine the missing number using addition strategies. *Note:* Do not suggest subtraction—this is an addition problem!

Students could use strategies like counting up, one-to-one correspondence or matching to find the solution. If students see for themselves the idea of using subtraction to find the missing addend and can explain the process, then you can use the strategy. Keep in mind that this is an example of a strategy, not a procedure.

Show students how to compare the two numbers to find the solution by taking the four studs off the left ten-frame and placing them on top of the seven studs that show the sum. The number of studs uncovered (3) reveals the number of studs needed in the change location.

Have students draw the model and explain the parts of the problem.

Students should understand that the start number is 4. Counting up from 4 ("5, 6, 7") uses three numbers. This shows that the missing addend is 3. The sum is 7.

2. Show students this addition problem: $5 + \boxed{} = 9$

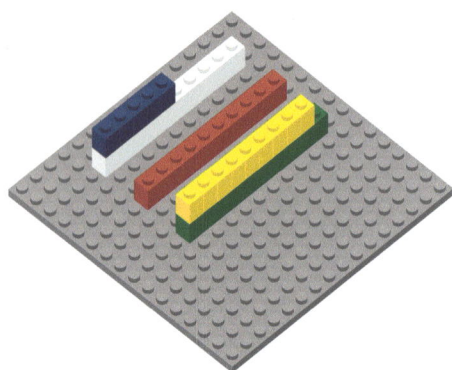

Ask students how to go about finding the missing number (*addend*) that belongs in the box.

Show students how to model the problem. Build three 1x10 strips or ten-frames to represent the three numbers in the problem (the two addends and the sum). *Note:* 1x10 strip models are shown for this problem.

Place 5 studs on the left strip to represent the addend in the starting place.

Do not place any studs on the center strip to represent the missing addend in the change location.

Place 9 studs on the right strip to represent the sum.

Ask students how to use this model to find the solution. Students could compare the starting addend to the sum to determine the change unknown addend. Another method is to take the 5 bricks representing the starting number and place them on the 9 bricks representing the sum, and then count up to fill the spots, "6, 7, 8, 9," showing that 4 numbers are needed to make the sum.

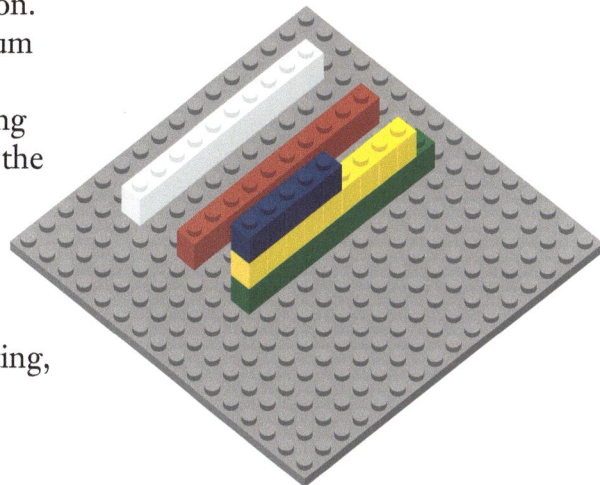

Have students draw the model and describe it in writing, showing both addends and the sum.

3. Show students this addition problem: $2 + \boxed{} = 8$

Ask students how to go about finding the missing number (*addend*) that belongs in the box.

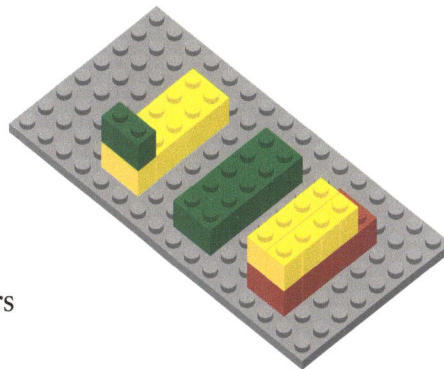

Show students how to model the problem. Build three 1x10 strips or ten-frames to represent the three numbers in the problem (the two addends and the sum). *Note:* Ten-frame models are shown for this problem.

Place 2 studs on the left ten-frame to represent the addend in the starting place.

Do not place any studs on the center ten-frame to represent the missing addend in the change location.

Place 8 studs on the right ten-frame to represent the sum.

Create a comparison model to show the solution. Move the 2 studs representing the first addend on top of the 8 bricks representing the sum, to show 6 uncovered studs as the solution.

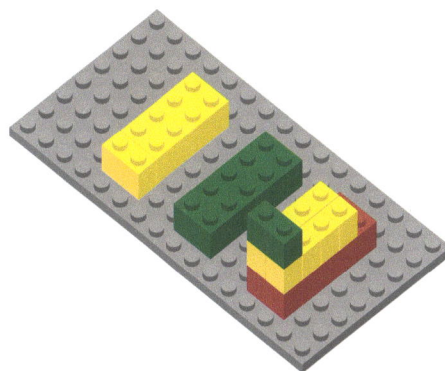

Ask students how to use this model to find the solution. Students could compare the starting addend to the sum to determine the change unknown addend. Another method is to take the 2 bricks representing the starting number and place them on the 8 bricks representing the sum, and then count up to fill the spots, "3, 4, 5, 6, 7, 8," showing that 6 numbers are needed to make the sum.

Have students draw the model and describe it in writing, showing both addends and the sum.

Part 2: Show What You Know

1. Can you build a model that shows this math sentence?

$3 + \boxed{} = 5$

You can use a 1x10 strip model or a ten-frame model. Draw your model.

Possible models:

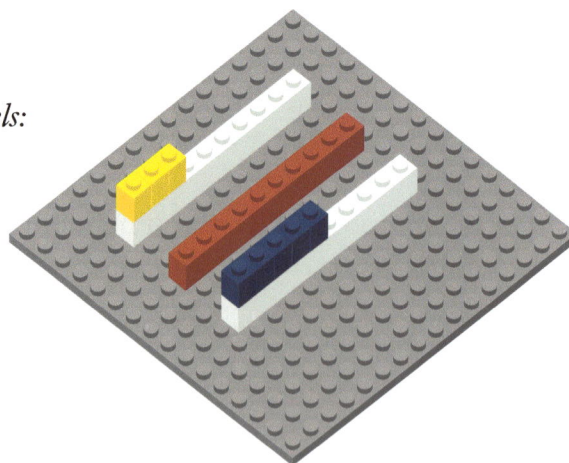

On your model, show how to find the missing addend.
Draw your solution.

Possible models:

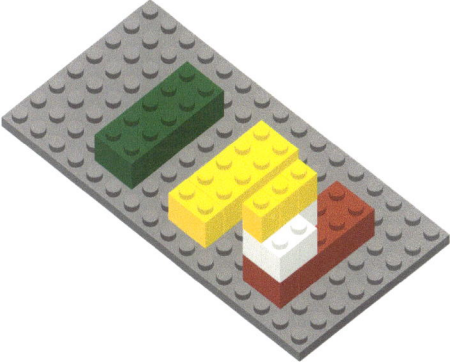

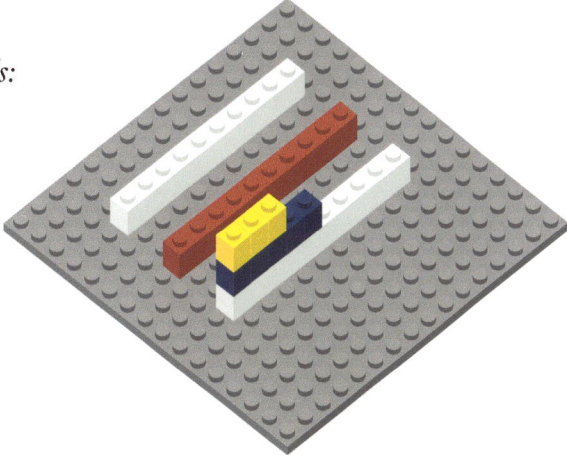

Model all three parts of the problem. Draw your model.
Label the addends and the sum.

Suggested solutions:

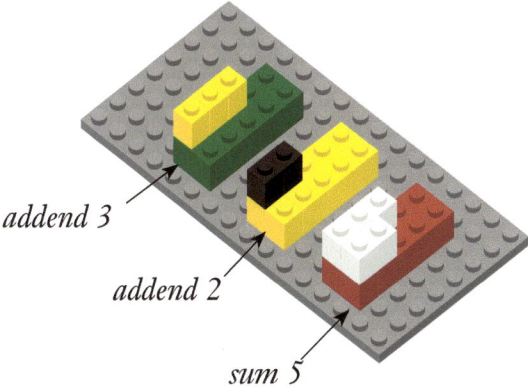

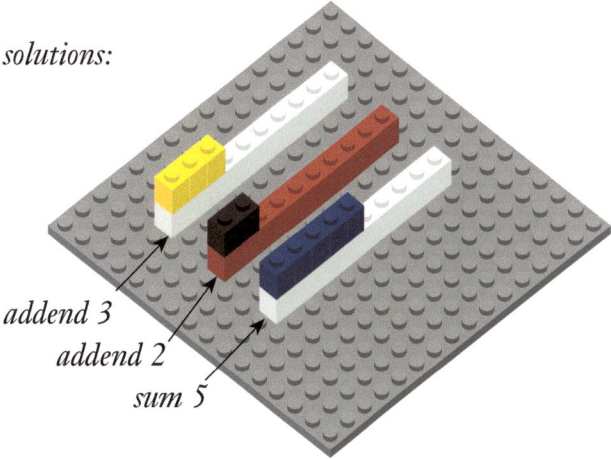

addend 3

addend 2

sum 5

addend 3

addend 2

sum 5

2. Can you build a model that shows this math sentence?

$$8 + \boxed{} = 10$$

You can use a 1x10 model or a ten-frame model. Draw your model.

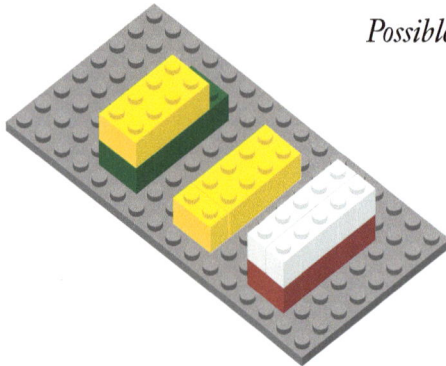

Possible models:

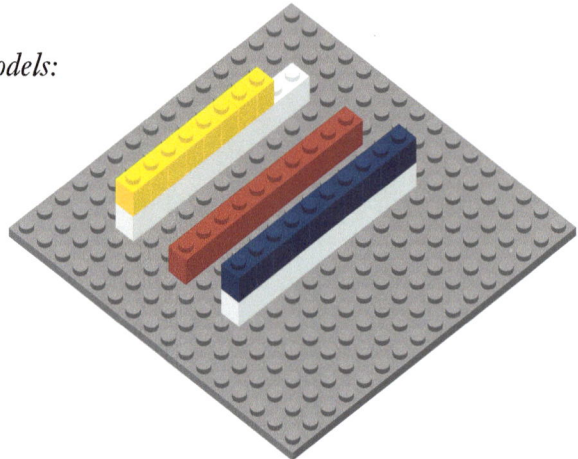

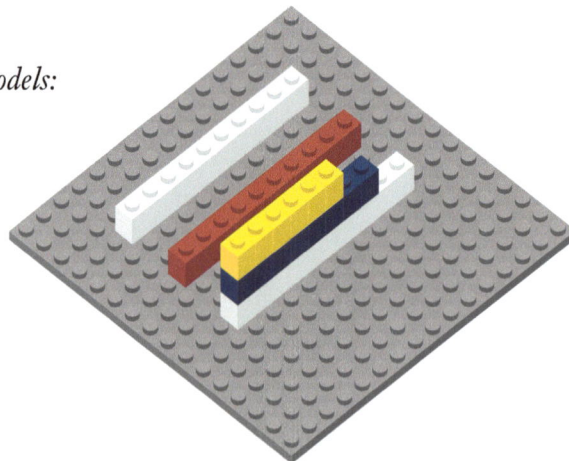

On your model, show how to find the missing addend. Draw your solution.

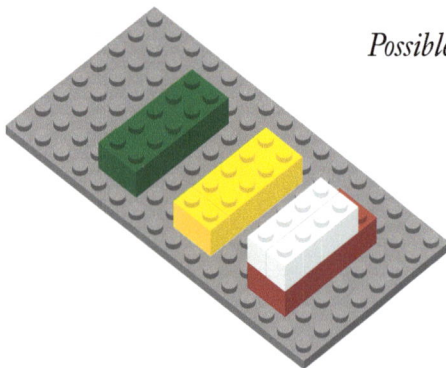

Possible models:

Answer: The model shows two studs uncovered in the sum, which proves that the change unknown addend is 2.

Model all three parts of the problem. Draw your model.
Label the addends and the sum.

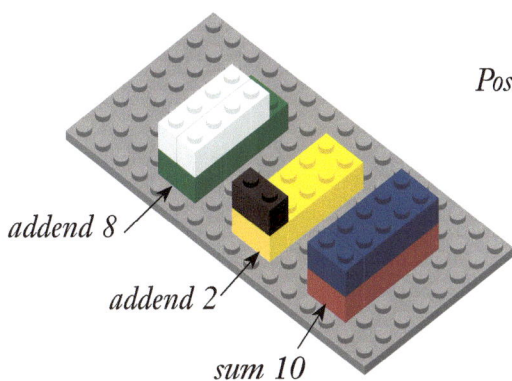

Possible models:

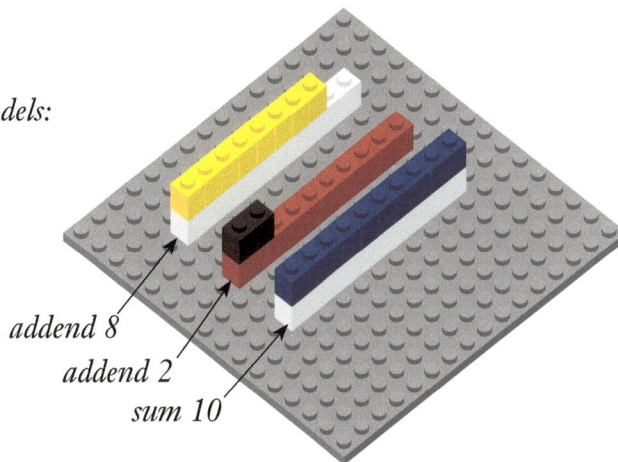

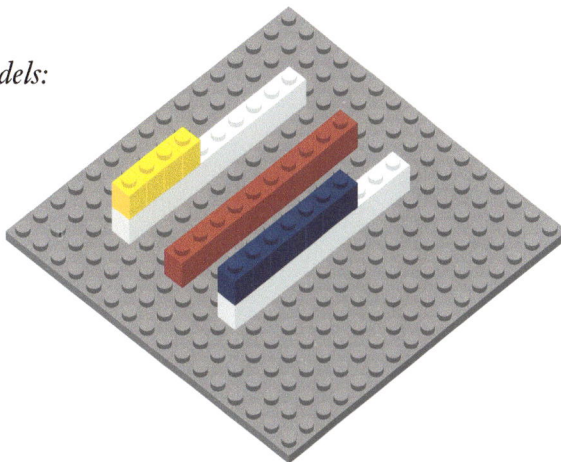

addend 8

addend 2

sum 10

addend 8

addend 2

sum 10

3. Can you build a model for this math sentence?

4 + ☐ = 7

You can use a 1x10 model or a ten-frame model. Draw
your model.

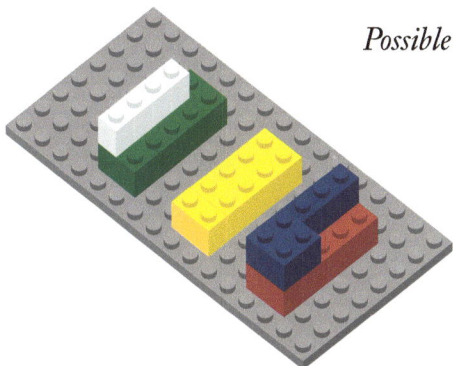

Possible models:

On your model, show how to find the missing addend. Draw your solution.

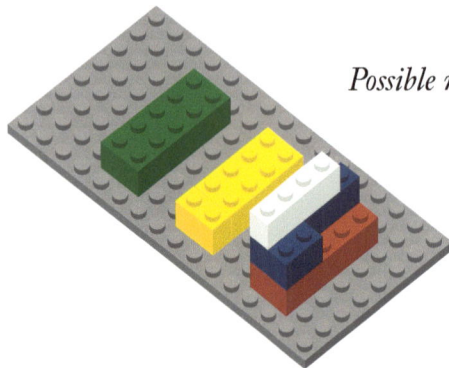

Possible models:

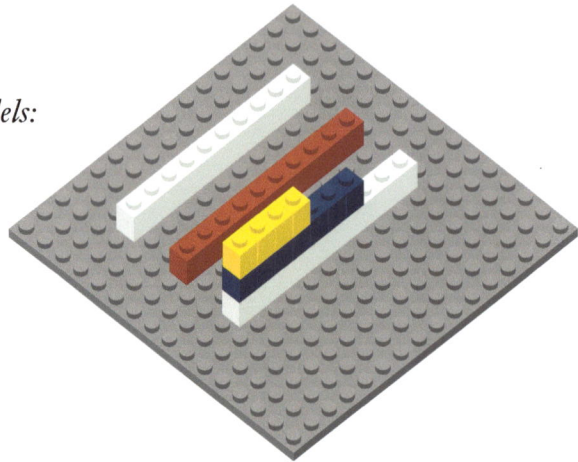

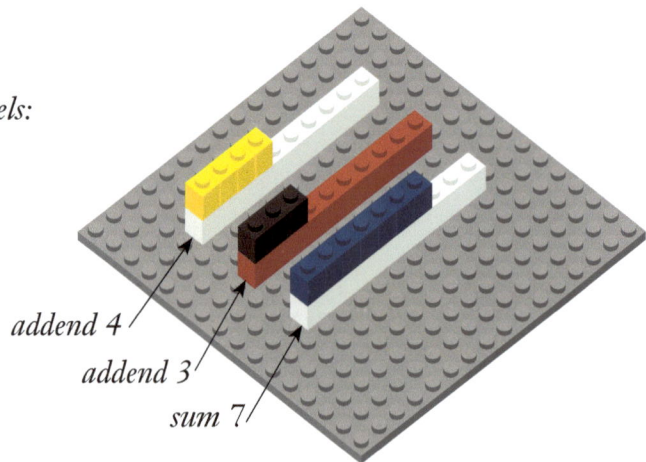

Answer: This model shows 3 studs uncovered in the sum, which proves that the change unknown addend is 3.

Model all three parts of the problem. Draw your model. Label the addends and the sum.

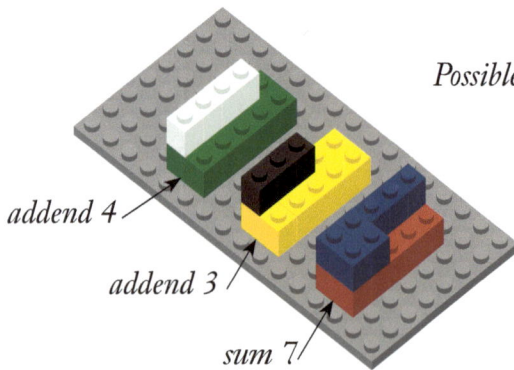

Possible models:

addend 4
addend 3
sum 7

addend 4
addend 3
sum 7

Challenge:

Can you build a model to show this math sentence?

$6 + \boxed{} = 13$

Hint: You will need more than 10 studs.

START UNKNOWN PROBLEMS

Students will learn/discover:
- How to solve problems where the starting number in the problem is unknown

Why is this important?

Being able to model different types of addition problems is key to understanding what strategies are best to utilize when solving each type. This lesson begins with the simplest problem type, start unknown, because this the first type of addition problem young mathematicians encounter as they begin the addition math journey.

Vocabulary:
- Add
- Join together
- Altogether
- Combined
- Start unknown

How to use the companion student book, *Learning Addition Using LEGO® Bricks*:
- After students build their models, have them draw the models and explain their thinking in the student book. Recording the models on paper after building them with bricks helps reinforce the concepts being taught.
- Discuss the vocabulary for each lesson with students as they work through the student book.
- Use the assessment in the student book to gauge student understanding of the content.

SUGGESTED BRICKS

Size	Number
1x1	10 each of 4 colors
1x2	6
1x3	6
1x4	5
2x2	5
2x3	5
2x4	5
1x10	3

Note: Using a baseplate will help keep the bricks in a uniform line. One large baseplate is suggested for these activities.

Note: The bricks used in these exercises may vary depending on students' ability to count. For example, if a student can see that a 1x3 brick is the same as three 1x1 bricks, they may use either configuration to show the number 3.

Part 1: Show Them How

1. Show students this addition problem: ⬚ + 3 = 7

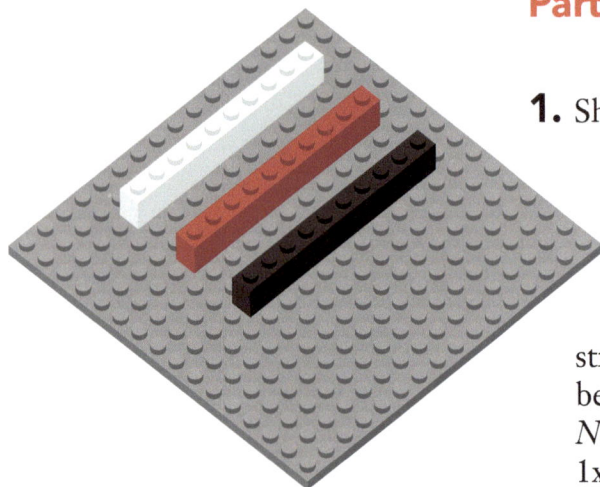

Ask students how to find the missing number (addend) that belongs in the box.

Show how to model the problem. Build three 1x10 strips or three ten-frames to represent the three numbers in the problem (the two addends and the sum). *Note:* Choose the modeling method that you prefer. The 1x10 strip method of modeling is illustrated here.

1x10 strips

2. Do not place any studs on the left strip, since the box in the math sentence is empty and the term is still unknown. Place 3 studs on the center strip to represent the addend 3 in the change location of the problem. Place 7 studs on the right strip to represent the sum.

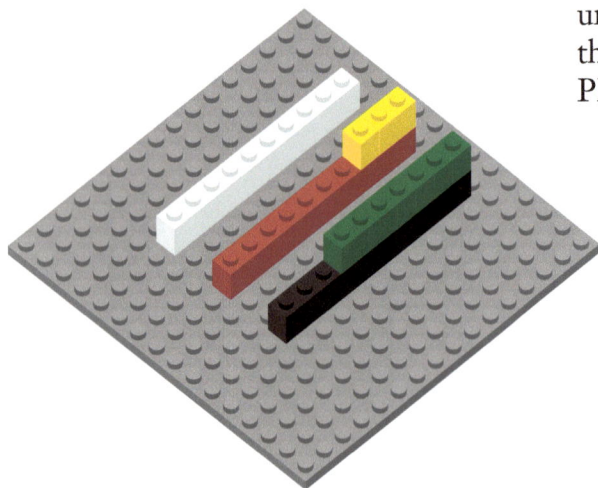

⬚ *+ 3 = 7*

3. Ask students how to determine the starting number using addition strategies. *Note:* You are looking for students to suggest addition strategies. Students could use strategies like counting on, one-to-one correspondence, or matching to find the solution. Once students see for themselves the idea of using subtraction to find the missing addend and can explain the process, then it is fine to use the strategy of subtraction. Keep in mind that you want to discuss a strategy for solving at this time, not a procedure.

4. Show students how to compare the two numbers to find the solution. Take 3 more studs that are the same as the ones on the center strip and stack them on top of the right strip that shows the sum. The number of studs uncovered reveals the number of studs needed on the left strip.

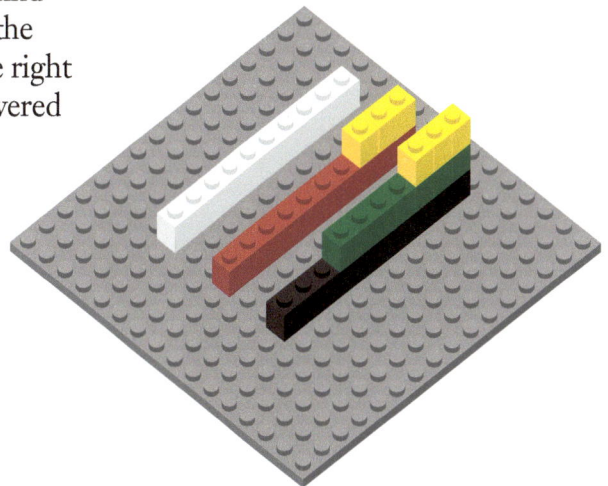

5. Model the solution.

To prove the solution, take the 4 studs from the left strip and the 3 studs from the center strip and stack them on top of the 7 studs on the right strip. This shows that the sum is equivalent to the parts of the problem.

Note: This is important as young learners begin to focus on part-part-whole relationships in problems.

Have students draw the model of the addends and the sum. Have students explain the parts of the problem.

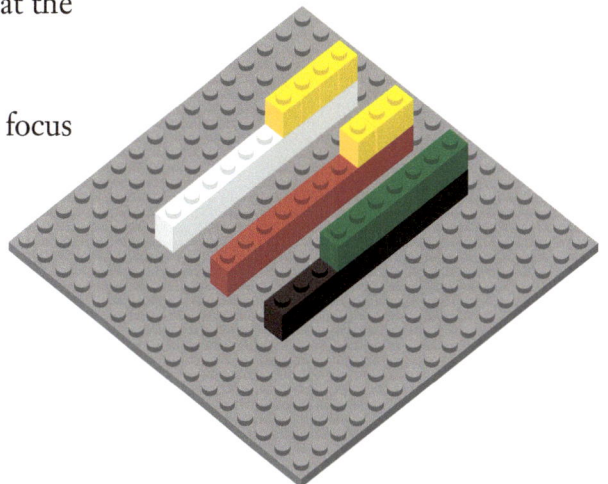

$$\boxed{4} + 3 = 7$$

6. Model the problem: $\boxed{}$ + 7 = 10

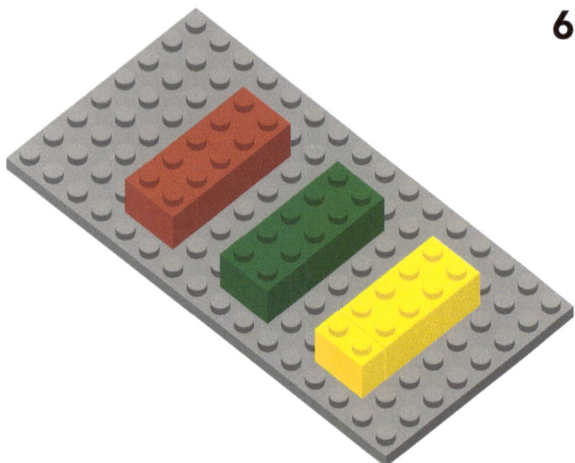

Build a 1x10 strip model or a ten-frame model. *Note:* Choose the method you prefer. The ten-frame method of modeling is illustrated here.

Ask students how to find the missing number (addend) that belongs in the box. Model the problem and have students create the same model.

Ask students what each part of the model represents. Students should answer that the left and center ten-frames represent the addends and the right ten-frame represents the sum.

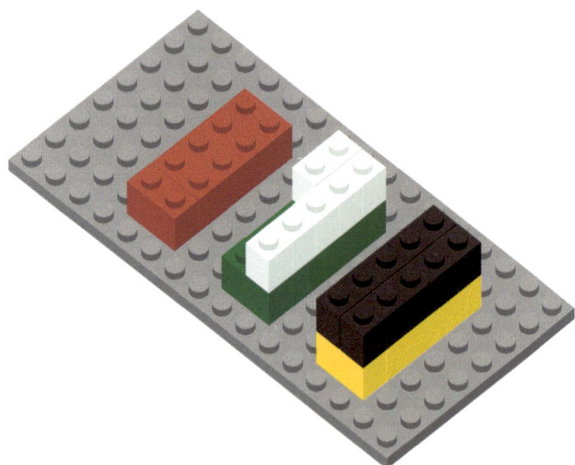

Don't place any studs on the left ten-frame, since the box in the math sentence is empty and still unknown. Place 7 studs on the center ten-frame to represent the addend 7 in the change location. Place 10 studs on the right ten-frame to represent the sum.

7. Ask students how to determine the starting number using addition strategies. Students could use strategies like counting up, one-to-one correspondence or comparison matching to find the solution.

Show students how to compare the two numbers to find the solution by placing the 7 bricks from the center ten-frame on top of the ten-frame that shows the sum. The number of bricks uncovered (3) reveals the number of studs needed on the left ten-frame.

Show students how to count up or use one-to-one correspondence to find the solution. Count the studs as you place each stud on top of the sum when you are comparing. After you say the number "7" and place the seventh stud, count "8, 9, 10" of the missing studs.

Have students draw the model of the addends and the sum, and explain the parts of the problem.

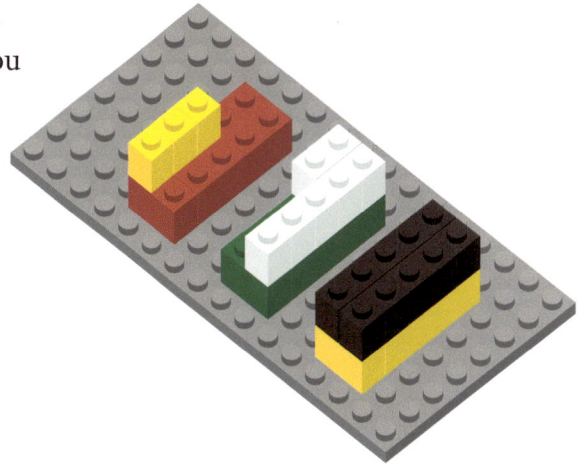

Part 2: Show What You Know

1. Can you model this problem? ☐ + 4 = 6

Step 1: Build the model frame. Use either a 1x10 strip model or a ten-frame model. Outline the frame on baseplate paper.

Step 2: Model the addend and the sum (4 and 6). Draw the model.

Step 3: Show all three numbers in the problem in your model and explain how you found the missing addend.

Students could use one of the strategies such as counting on, comparing, or counting up. Students should show 2 as the missing addend.

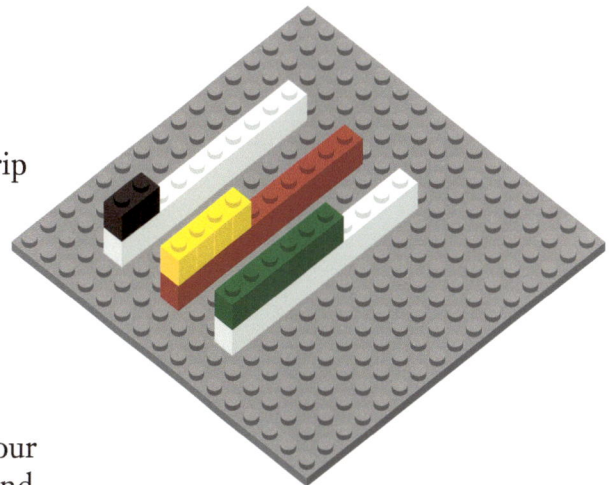

2 + 4 = 6

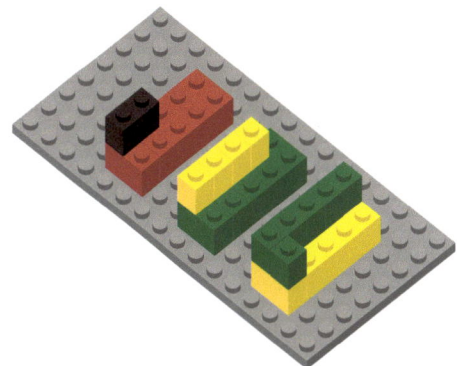

2 + 4 = 6

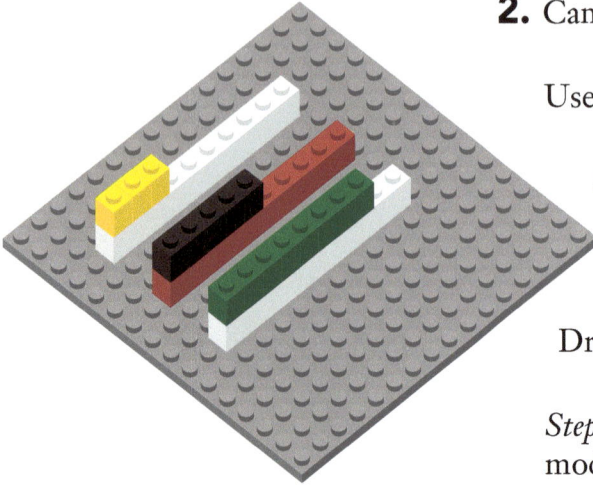

2. Can you model this problem? ☐ + 5 = 8

Use either a 1x10 strip model or a ten-frame model.

> *Step 1*: Build the model frame. Outline the frame on baseplate paper.

> *Step 2*: Model the addend and the sum (5 and 8). Draw your model of this step.

Step 3: Show all three numbers in the problem in your model and explain how you found the missing addend.

Students could use one of the strategies such as counting on, comparing, or counting up. Students should show 3 as the missing addend.

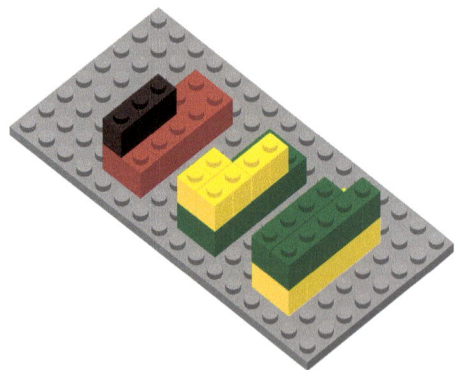

3 + 5 = 8

3. Can you model this problem? ☐ + 6 = 9

Use either a 1x10 strip model or a ten-frame model.

Step 1: Build the model frame. Outline the frame on baseplate paper.

Step 2: Model the addend and the sum (6 and 9). Draw your model of this step.

Step 3: Show all three numbers in the problem in your model and explain how you found the missing addend.

Students could use one of the strategies such as counting on, comparing, or counting up. Students should show 3 as the missing addend.

3 + 6 = 9

SUGGESTED BRICKS

Size	Number
1x1	10 each of 4 colors
1x2	16
1x3	4

Note: Using a baseplate will help keep the bricks in a uniform line. One large baseplate is suggested for these activities.

ADDING LARGER NUMBERS

Students will learn/discover:
- How to add numbers to sums within 100 using a place value method

Why is this important?
Being able to add numbers that are sums within 100 begins the process of adding even larger numbers. Linking place value to addition and decomposing numbers is key to understanding the way addition is related to other operations.

Vocabulary:
- Add: To join together
- Sum: The solution to an addition problem
- Addend: Each of the numbers being added together in an addition problem
- Compose: To bring together parts of a number into a whole
- Decompose: To break a number into parts that make up a whole. This is usually referred to as *regrouping* when working with base ten.

How to use the companion student book, *Learning Addition Using LEGO*® Bricks:
- After students build their models, have them draw the models and explain their thinking in the student book. Recording the models on paper after building them with bricks helps reinforce the concepts being taught.
- Discuss the vocabulary for each lesson with students as they work through the student book.
- Use the assessment in the student book to gauge student understanding of the content.

Part 1: Show Them How

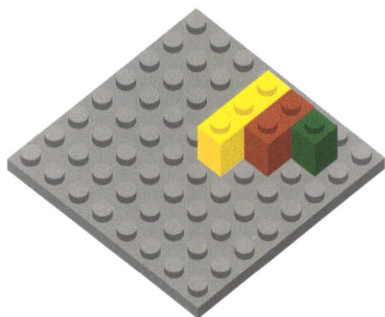

1. Show students how to build a place value model. Point out the representational value of each brick in the model. The 1x1 brick represents the ones; the 1x2 brick represents the tens; the 1x3 brick represents the hundreds.

2. Have students build the number 22 using two 1x2 bricks (representing 20) and two 1x1 bricks (representing 2).

   Have students build the number 11 using one 1x2 brick (representing 10) and one 1x1 brick (representing 1).

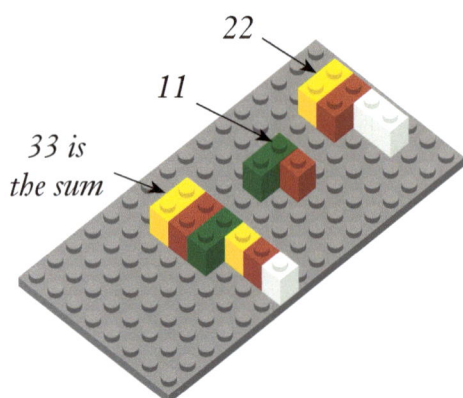

3. Show students how to compose (join) these two numbers and form a new model that represents the sum. Have students build a third model to show the composing action and then draw and label their solution.

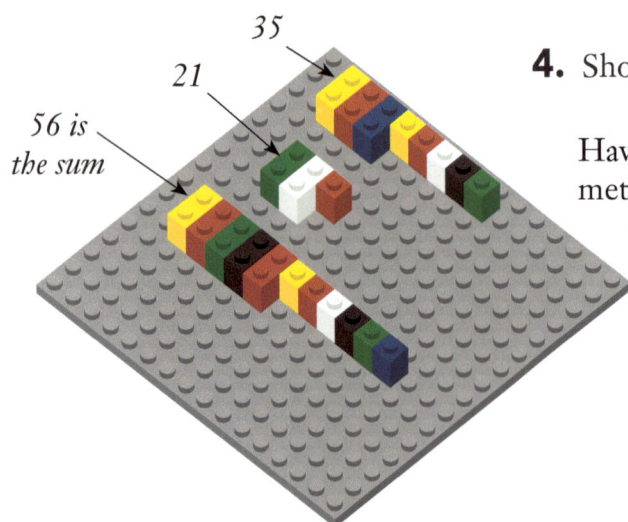

4. Show students this math sentence: 35 + 21 = ☐

   Have students build each number using the place value method. Show how to combine the two addends to compose the sum. Have students build the model that composes the sum and then draw and label their solutions.

5. Show students this math sentence: 62 + 24 = ☐

Build each of the addends. Show the composing of the bricks to form the sum. Have students build the model that composes the sum and then draw and label their solutions.

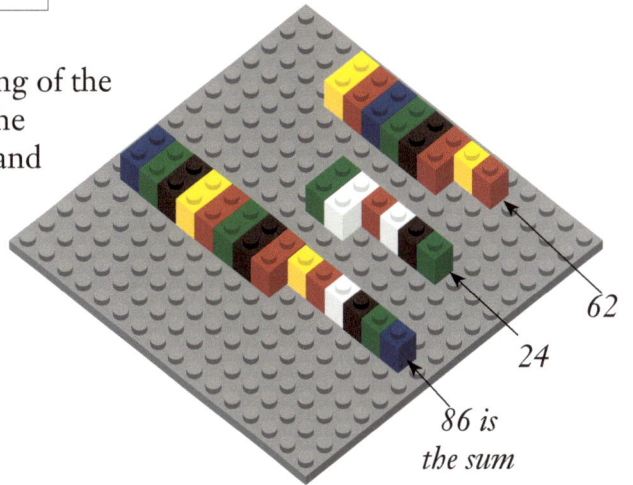

62

24

86 is the sum

Part 2: Show What You Know

1. Can you build a model to show the addition of 33 + 44? Build a model of the sum. Draw and label the model.

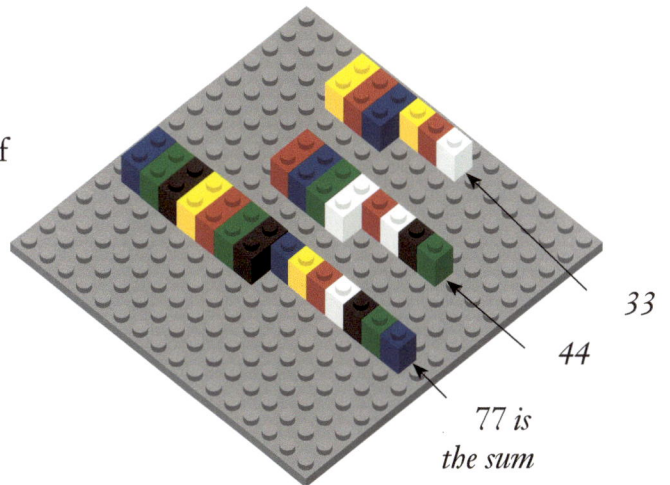

33

44

77 is the sum

56

33

89 is the sum

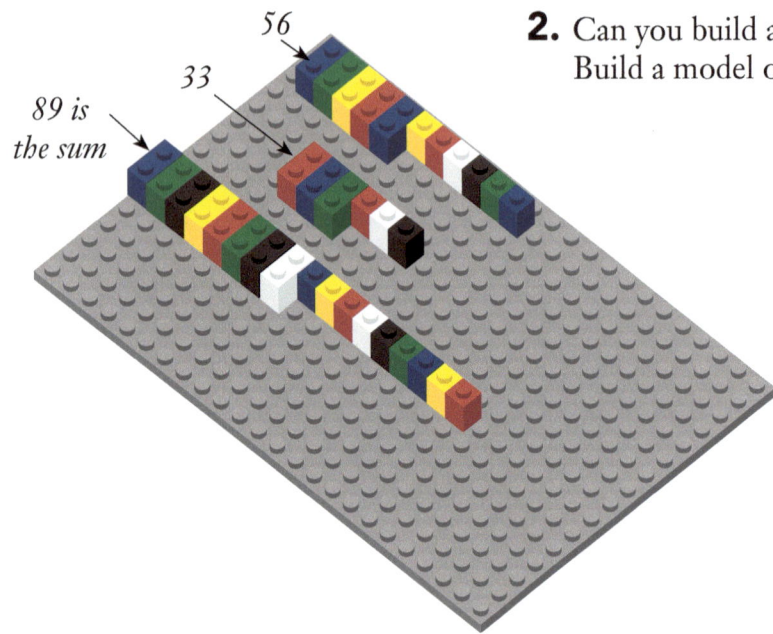

2. Can you build a model to show the addition of 56 + 33? Build a model of the sum. Draw and label the model.

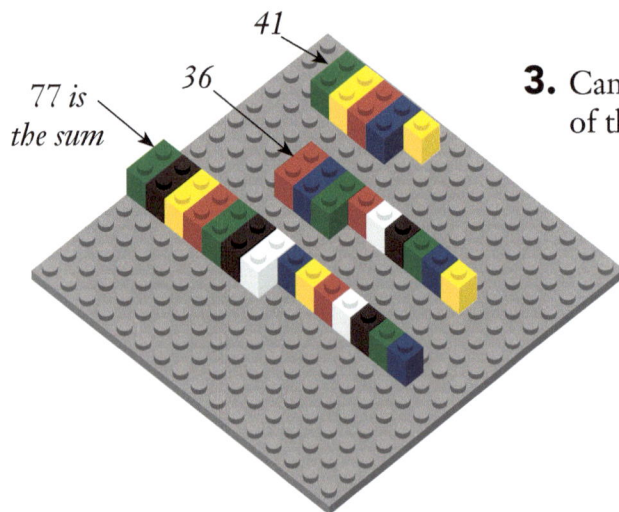

41

36

77 is the sum

3. Can you build a model to show 41 + 36? Build a model of the sum. Draw and label the model.

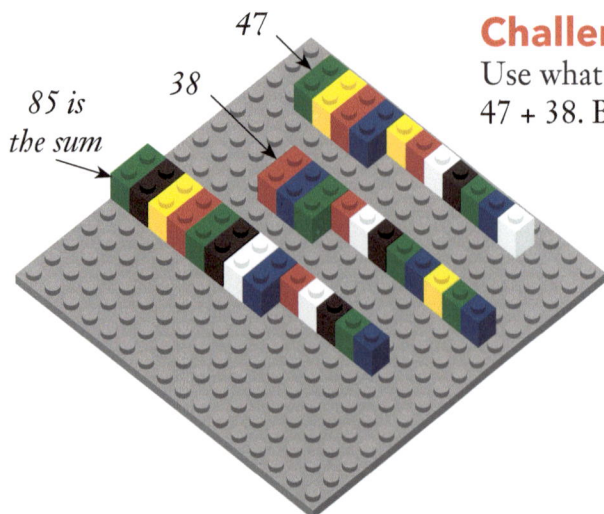

47

38

85 is the sum

Challenge:

Use what you know about decomposing to find the sum of 47 + 38. Build a model, then draw and label it.

APPENDIX

- **Suggested Brick Inventory**
- **Student Assessment Chart**
- **Baseplate Paper**

SUGGESTED BRICK INVENTORY

SIZE	NUMBER
1x1	84 (32 each of two colors and 10 each of two more colors)
1x2	25 (10 each of two colors and 5 of a third color)
1x3	12 (6 each of two colors)
1x4	10
1x6	10
1x8	6
1x10	6
1x12	5
1x16	2
2x2	12
2x3	6
2x4	9
2x6	4
2x8	2
2x10	2

ADDITION
Student Assessment Chart

Name _____

Performance Skill	Not yet	With help	On target	Comments
I can model addition problems using hundreds, tens, and ones.				
I can show and tell what it means to add numbers.				
I can add within 20.				
I can model how to find the first missing addend (start unknown) in an addition problem.				
I can model how to find the second missing addend (change unknown) in an addition problem.				
I can model how to find the missing result in an addition problem.				
I can decompose numbers to make sets of tens and ones.				
I can model many ways to make the same number.				
I can use place value and decomposing to add larger numbers up to 100.				

BASEPLATE PAPER

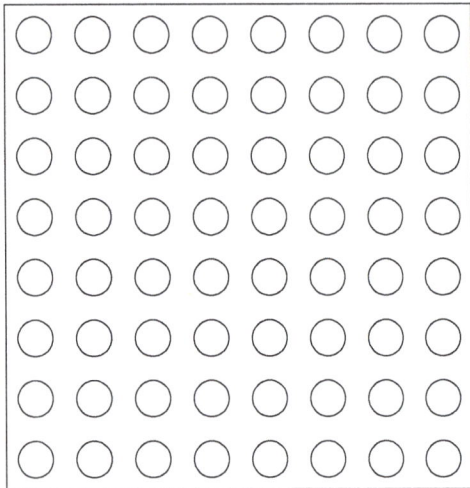

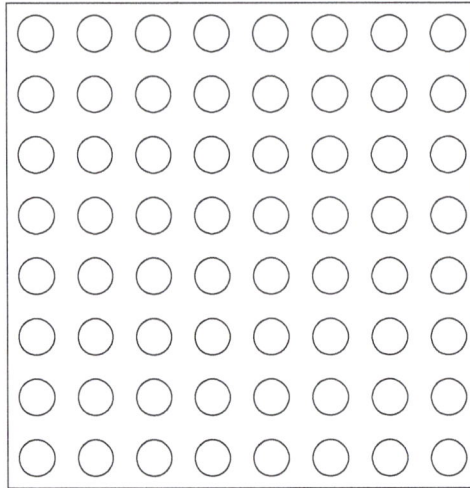

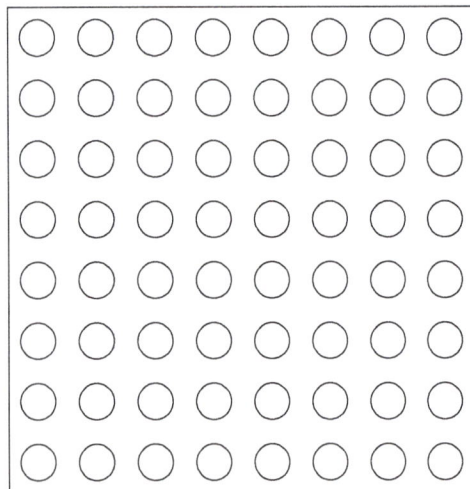

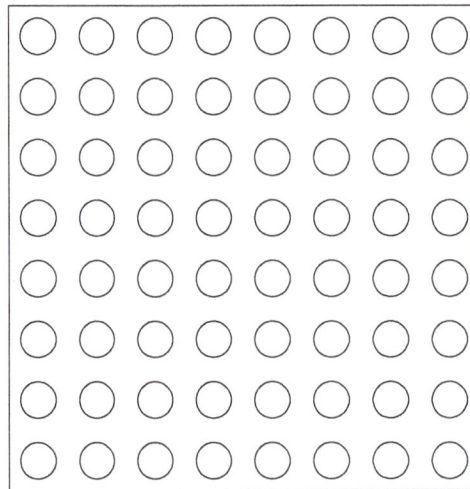

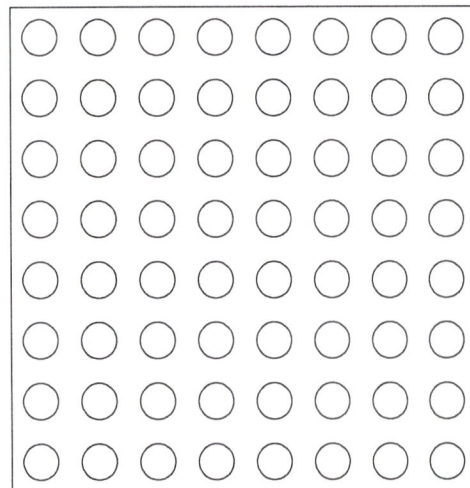

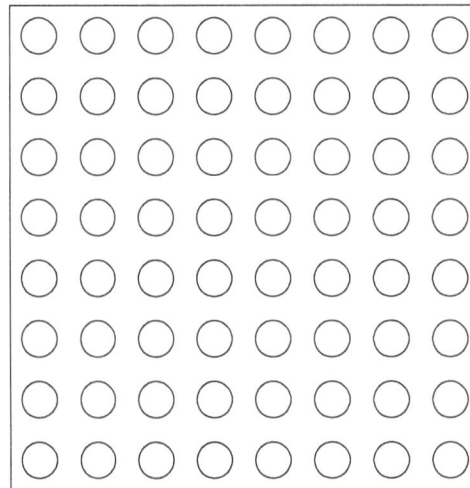

BASEPLATE PAPER

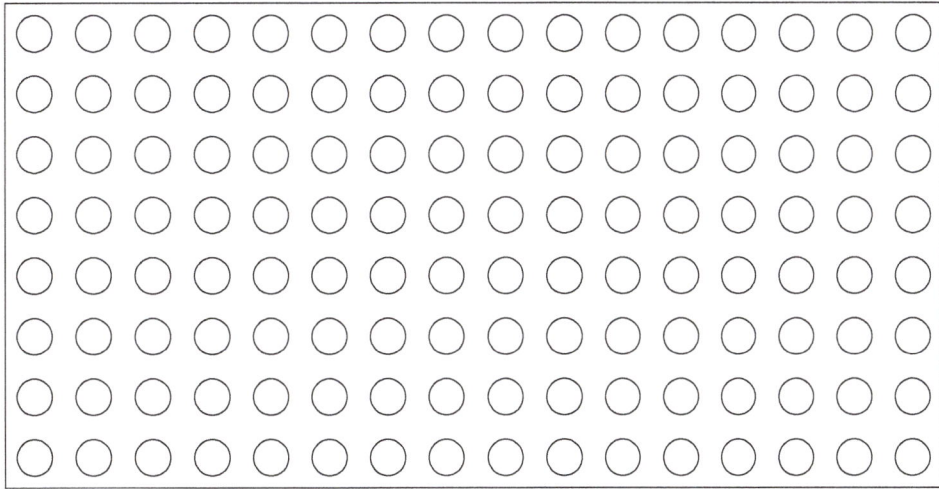

Brick Math Series:
TEACHING MATH USING LEGO® BRICKS
www.brick-math.com

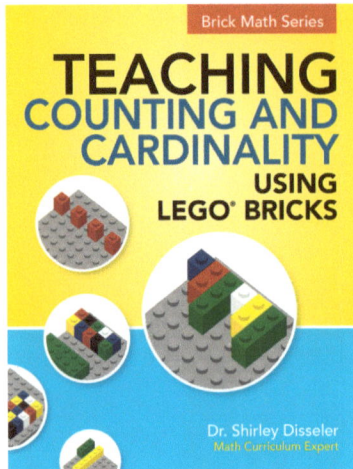

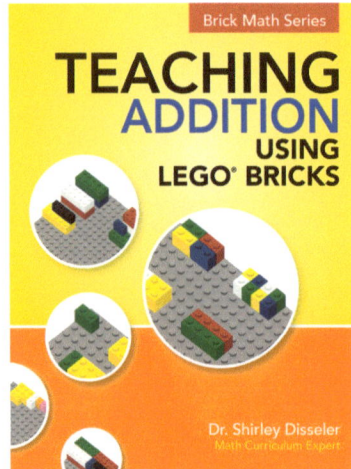

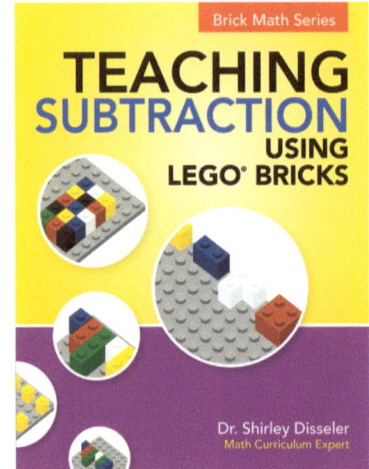

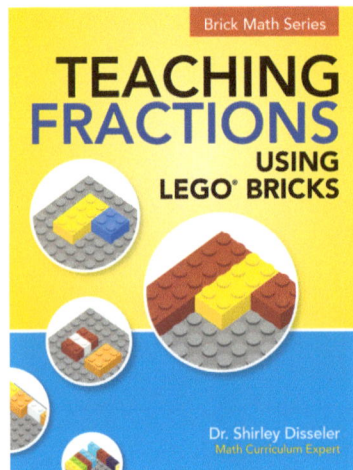

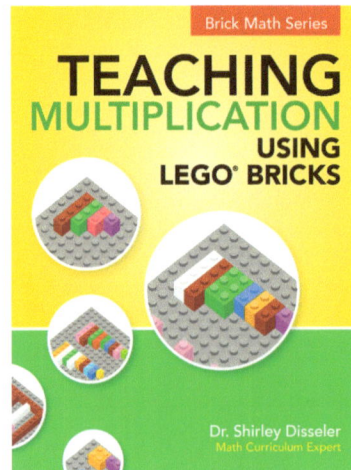

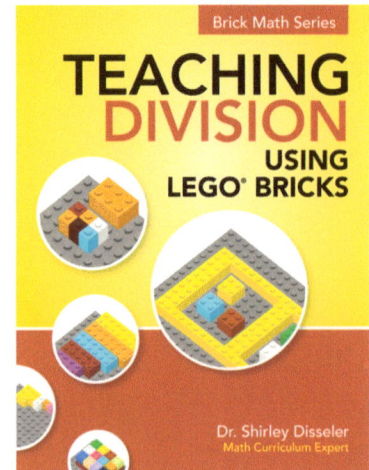

Brick Math Series

TEACHING COUNTING AND CARDINALITY USING LEGO® BRICKS

Dr. Shirley Disseler
Math Curriculum Expert

Brick Math Series

TEACHING ADDITION USING LEGO® BRICKS

Dr. Shirley Disseler
Math Curriculum Expert

Brick Math Series

TEACHING SUBTRACTION USING LEGO® BRICKS

Dr. Shirley Disseler
Math Curriculum Expert

Brick Math Series

TEACHING FRACTIONS USING LEGO® BRICKS

Dr. Shirley Disseler
Math Curriculum Expert

Brick Math Series

TEACHING MULTIPLICATION USING LEGO® BRICKS

Dr. Shirley Disseler
Math Curriculum Expert

Brick Math Series

TEACHING DIVISION USING LEGO® BRICKS

Dr. Shirley Disseler
Math Curriculum Expert

Companion Student Editions
Individual student books that follow the teaching curriculum, complete with additional activities for practice and assessments.

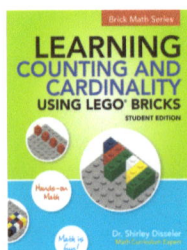

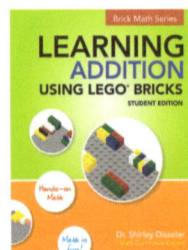

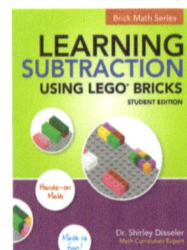

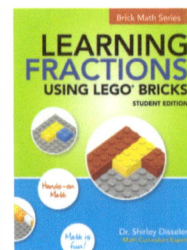

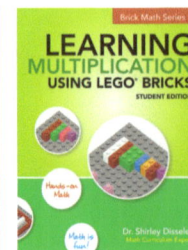

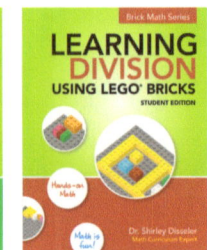

Brick Math Series

LEARNING COUNTING AND CARDINALITY USING LEGO® BRICKS

Hands-on Math

Made in fun!

Dr. Shirley Disseler
Math Curriculum Expert

Brick Math Series

LEARNING ADDITION USING LEGO® BRICKS

Dr. Shirley Disseler

Brick Math Series

LEARNING SUBTRACTION USING LEGO® BRICKS

Dr. Shirley Disseler

Brick Math Series

LEARNING FRACTIONS USING LEGO® BRICKS
STUDENT EDITION

Made in fun!

Dr. Shirley Disseler
Math Curriculum Expert

Brick Math Series

LEARNING MULTIPLICATION USING LEGO® BRICKS
STUDENT EDITION

Dr. Shirley Disseler
Math Curriculum Expert

Brick Math Series

LEARNING DIVISION USING LEGO® BRICKS
STUDENT EDITION

Dr. Shirley Disseler
Math Curriculum Expert